What Makes A Hater

Ralph Nyadzi

Published by Cegast Academy, 2024.

While every precaution has been taken in the preparation of this book, the publisher assumes no responsibility for errors or omissions, or for damages resulting from the use of the information contained herein.

WHAT MAKES A HATER

First edition. July 12, 2024.

Copyright © 2024 Ralph Nyadzi.

ISBN: 979-8227781772

Written by Ralph Nyadzi.

Also by Ralph Nyadzi

Fast Track WASSCE General Arts
Fast Track WASSCE Government: Elements of Government

Standalone
Regrets
The Self-Support Guide
Becoming Self-Employed
Understanding Grammatical Names and Functions
Second Class Citizen Summary & Analysis
The Lion and the Jewel Summary & Analysis
WAEC Literature Poetry: Summary & Analysis
WAEC Literature African Poetry Summary & Analysis
WAEC Literature Non-African Poetry Summary & Analysis
What Makes A Hater

Watch for more at https://www.cegastacademy.com.

Table of Contents

Preface and Book Overview

"Still I Rise", by Maya Angelou

You may write me down in history
With your bitter, twisted lies,
You may trod me in the very dirt
But still, like dust, I'll rise.

- Personal stories about dealing with jealousy, envy and haters

- Importance of addressing jealousy, envy and hatred in modern society

- Book overview and what you will gain from the book

3 Personal Stories

Like almost everyone reading this book, I've had my fair share of envy, jealousy and hatred since childhood. But the ones I will share with you are significant because each nearly derailed my plans for achieving a better life for myself and those I care about.

EXTENDED FAMILY HATERS

So I'll begin with the place closest to me – family. I was born to parents who, though they didn't go far in formal education, were exceptional pupils in their schooldays. So, naturally, my siblings and I have that gift in our blood. My brothers and I, in particular, left lasting impressions wherever we went to school. But for some reason, many of our cousins from the paternal side couldn't match us in any way. This set the stage for jealousy and open hatred towards us. The interesting part of all this is that despite our academic brilliance, our parents didn't have the means to pay for the kind of secondary education that would bring out the best in us. Our individual chance circumstances backed by our determination to put what the Creator has endowed us with to good use saw us progressing to the discomfort of the haters. To cut a long story short, we did our best, but the toxic atmosphere of jealousy and envy, marked sometimes by deliberate acts to derail our plans, have combined to make life almost unbearable for us even up to this day. It is from this first-hand encounter with jealousy and envy that I came to appreciate the extent to which haters and envious people can hurt anyone who they consider to be 'better' than them.

THE EXAM MALPRACTICE CONSPIRACY

My second significant encounter with jealous people came when I started work as a trained teacher at a time I was in my early twenties. Once again, it was my show of academic brilliance and an ambition to climb the educational ladder that made some of my colleagues turn against me. Do not get me wrong. I've never been the arrogant or boastful type. In everything I do or say, I'm guided by the reality of my very humble background. But haters don't care about that. So once again, a conspiracy was hatched to land me in trouble with the external examination management board in my country and the law enforcement agencies. For weeks after news got around that the police were arresting middle school Form 4 teachers who assisted their students in engaging in exam malpractices, I was on my knees praying that the Universe would let the authorities see my innocence in the matter. Who did I have to come and bail me out when my parents were far away in a different part of the country and were in no position, financially, to pay the kind of money others had to cough up to be set free from the police cell? It took my reputation of integrity and divine intervention to escape from the trap set by my haters. One official from the District Education office who accompanied the police to my school jumped to my defence as I entered the headteacher's office where they had invited me. He told everyone present: 'This guy would never do such a thing'. Here is the thing. Sometime before all this started, I encountered this man (who later became a District Chief Executive) during an in-service training workshop. An incident occurred where I openly displayed my dislike for underhand dealings in any form. He later told me my behaviour left a lasting impression on him and I'm grateful to him. Later in my school, I held fast to my principles of honesty and hard work when the trap was being prepared for me. That was what saved me. Maybe one day in the future I will provide the details in another book so you can understand better.

THE MISSING UNIVERSITY ADMISSION LETTER

Within a couple of years after the above incident, I had an admission to the university. At this time, I had obtained a transfer to a different school in a different town. But for some reason, I continued to attract haters and jealous people. This time, the big one had to do with my university admission letter. As I now write about this episode, the whereabouts of my original admission letter remain a mystery. I never had access to that admission letter. It got picked up in the post and whoever took it made sure it never reached me.

I'm speaking of the early 1990s when admission letters were still being sent to qualified applicants by post. Someone in a nearby town had to take delivery of my school's letters and distribute them to the rightful owners. That was where my admission letter got missing in transit. Someone decided that I was not fit to go to university so I didn't need that admission letter.

I know you will be asking so how come I attended university anyway? Here is what happened. It was a time in my life when all my mind and thoughts were focused on one thing only: Gaining admission to university despite all the roadblocks that made it almost impossible for someone with my background to achieve such a dream. Being always conscious of this, I never left anything to chance. When a few days went by and I didn't hear anything from the university I applied to, I took matters into my own hands. I travelled to the university to meet the authorities. At first, they put my failure to receive an admission letter to the fact that I never qualified and was never admitted in the first place. That was why no letter was sent to me. But I was sure I had the grades needed for admission. I refused to back down and leave. Finally, one secretary suggested to the registrar that they go through the files to verify my claims. Lo and behold. There was my name in the first list of those admitted to the Faculty of Arts. All other records pointed to the fact that the letter had been duly posted to my address.

They gave me a new admission letter with all the blank spaces in it for me to fill out there and then. Thus, I wrote my own admission letter, so to speak. It was handed to those who had to sign it and they quickly did so. This then was how I got my second admission letter. The original one might still be with the hater who sat on it or destroyed it decades ago.

There is another angle to this story. It has to do with some mysterious circumstances surrounding my residential status as a freshman. I intend to tell you in my other book to show how the Universe intervenes in our lives in mysterious ways. So watch out for that book.

A SIMILAR STORY FROM NEW YORK CITY

This one is a familiar story recounting the writer's close encounter with jealousy.

In the bustling city of New York, my career was on a steady incline. I had just received a promotion at my job, my social circle was expanding, and I was about to launch a personal project I had been working on for years. Life seemed perfect, or so I thought. Little did I know, beneath the surface of my success, jealousy and envy were brewing among those I considered friends and colleagues. One incident, in particular, stands out—a close friend subtly began to undermine my achievements. She cleverly masked her envy with backhanded compliments and subtle jabs.

These real-life events marked the beginning of my journey to understanding and overcoming jealousy, both from others and within myself.

As you can see, haters and jealous people are always there to make life difficult for their victims. And where we fail to be conscious of the dangers they pose to our ambitions and happiness, they succeed and gloat about it. This book will show you many aspects of the virulent phenomena of jealousy, hatred and envy including how to overcome them in your endeavours.

Importance of Addressing Jealousy and Envy

Jealousy and envy are emotions as old as humanity itself, yet they remain some of the most challenging to deal with. In today's hyper-connected world, where social media platforms constantly showcase curated glimpses of other people's seemingly perfect lives, these feelings are more pervasive than ever. Jealousy, envy and hatred can erode your self-esteem, damage your relationships, and hinder personal and professional growth. These negative effects hold for both the individual exhibiting these emotions and anybody at the receiving end of their vendetta.

You need to bear in mind that addressing jealousy and envy is not just about managing these emotions in others. It is also about recognizing and mitigating them within ourselves.

Here is a reason for you to take what you're about to read in the coming chapters seriously: Understanding these feelings and learning how to deal with them can lead to healthier relationships, a more positive self-image, and greater overall well-being.

Book Overview

Here is what you must expect from this book.

The book is a comprehensive guide to understanding, addressing, and overcoming jealousy, envy and hatred in all aspects of life.

It is divided into five chapters and a conclusion. Each chapter explores a key aspect of these emotions.

Chapter 1: Understanding Jealousy, Envy and Hatred

Here are the insights you will gain about these emotions in the introductory chapter:

- Definitions and differences between jealousy, envy and hatred
- Psychological and emotional roots of jealousy and envy
- Historical and cultural perspectives on jealousy and envy
- How jealousy, envy and hatred are interconnected

Chapter 2: How to Spot Jealousy and Envy from Afar

This chapter will help you recognize the signs of jealousy and envy in yourself and others.

In this part, we will explore the reasons why you might attract haters and envious people. You will, therefore, gain an insight into the behaviour of anyone envious. Remember not all jealous people will show it to you openly. This part will equip you with that sixth sense to smell envy and jealousy from afar.

Chapter 3: The Impact of Jealousy and Envy.

Here, we will talk about the dangers that jealousy and envy pose to your goals, relationships, and professional life. Real-life examples and case studies will illustrate the significant impact these emotions can have.

Chapter 4: How to Overcome Jealousy and Envy

This segment gives you practical strategies for dealing with envious people and haters in your life. It also shows you what you need to do to overcome your own feelings of envy towards others.

Much of what you will learn here will increase your ability to work towards personal growth, emotional resilience, and effective communication.

Chapter 5: Long-Term Strategies for a Jealousy-Free, Envy-Free Life

The final part of the book provides long-term strategies for building emotional resilience. You will cultivate the habit of gratitude. From now on, you will know how to support others in overcoming jealousy.

The chapter emphasizes the importance of continuous self-improvement and the need to build and nurture a positive environment around your relationship with others.

By the end of this book, you will develop a deeper understanding of jealousy, envy and hatred, practical tools to manage these emotions, and strategies to thrive amidst negativity. You will be equipped to turn potential hindrances into opportunities for personal growth and transformation.

Conclusion

In this final section, I give you a summary of all the aspects of jealousy, envy and hatred you've been reading about. You will also find key resources that open the doors to additional help if you ever need one to overcome envy, jealousy and hatred.

What You Will Gain

After reading this book you will be empowered with the right knowledge and tools to achieve the following:

- Identify and understand jealousy, envy and hatred.

Learn to recognize these emotions in yourself and others, understand their roots, and gain a deep insight into the behaviour of those who are jealous.

- Manage and mitigate the impact of jealousy and envy.

Discover how jealousy and envy can create hatred and affect various aspects of your life. You will learn strategies to manage their impact on your aspirations, relationships, and career.

- Overcome jealousy and thrive

Develop personal growth strategies, build emotional resilience, and learn practical techniques for dealing with jealous people.

- Create a jealousy-free life

Implement long-term strategies for maintaining emotional health that build a spirit of gratitude, and support others in overcoming jealousy.

This book will not only help you deal with jealousy and envy but also pave the way for a more fulfilling, positive, and successful life.

Are you ready to learn how to overcome jealousy, envy and hatred in your life? Then come with me as we begin with Chapter 1: Understanding Jealousy, Envy and Hatred.

This chapter will provide the foundational knowledge that you and I need to clearly understand the psychological and emotional roots of these emotions.

PLEASE NOTE: I have deliberately used the terms 'jealousy' and 'envy' together with the resulting emotion of 'hate' or 'hatred' interchangeably throughout this book. My main reason is that, as you will soon realize, these emotions are very closely related and often combine to produce similar consequences in our lives. Thus, tackling one invariably amounts to dealing with the others as well.

A Poem for Inspiration

Dear Haters by Rupsa Chakraborty

You stand tall as an ice berg in my vogue.
You are the wildest storm in desert,
The toxic that burns my heart,
The madness that drives me insane.
But your hatred keeps me going.
I dare to go beyond my boundaries,
You imbibe new zest of inspiration,
I learn to conquer my fear,
Sail alone in the vast sea,
Your jealousy keep me sane.
Your words don't pierce...
Through my titanium heart...
Because I know haters only hate.
Hate me more to make me grow more.
With Love.

CONTINUE TO CHAPTER 1: UNDERSTANDING JEALOUSY, ENVY AND HATRED

Chapter 1: Understanding Jealousy, Envy and Hatred

- Definitions and differences between jealousy, envy and hatred
    - Psychological and emotional roots of jealousy and envy
    - Historical and cultural perspectives on jealousy and envy
    - How jealousy, envy and hatred are interconnected

Definitions and Differences Between Jealousy, Envy and Hatred

What is Jealousy?

Jealousy is often described as the fear of losing something you already have to someone else. It usually involves a triangle of relationships where one feels threatened by a rival. For instance, feeling jealous when your best friend spends more time with another friend, or when a romantic partner pays attention to someone else. A strong feeling of jealousy can elicit other negative reactions from us such as hateful thoughts and a desire to undermine or violently fight back.

What is Envy?

Envy, on the other hand, is the longing for something that someone else possesses. It involves two parties where one desires the qualities, achievements, or possessions of the other. For example, feeling envious of a colleague's promotion or a neighbour's luxurious lifestyle. The sad truth is that envy, if not managed properly, can also lead to the same reactions just as we saw a moment ago under jealousy.

What is Hatred?

Hatred is an intense feeling of dislike or animosity toward someone or something. It often involves a desire to harm or see harm come to the object of hate.

Psychological and Emotional Roots of Jealousy and Envy

According to ResearchGate[1], both jealousy and envy are deeply rooted in human psychology and emotions. Understanding their origins can help in managing these feelings more effectively.

Evolutionary Perspective

From an evolutionary standpoint, jealousy and envy may have developed as **survival mechanisms**. Jealousy could protect social bonds and family units.

Envy could serve as a **motivator for personal growth**. It has the potential to spur individuals to improve their status and acquire resources necessary for survival.

Low Self-Esteem and Insecurity

Low self-esteem and feelings of insecurity often fuel jealousy and envy. When individuals perceive themselves as lacking or unworthy, they are more prone to compare themselves to others unfavourably. This will mark the beginning of these emotions.

Fear of Loss or the Scarcity Mindset

Jealousy stems from a fear of losing something valuable, whether it's affection, attention, or a prized possession. Envy is often driven by a scarcity mindset. It begins to manifest whenever we believe that resources, success, or happiness are limited and someone else's gain is our loss.

Social Comparison

The theory of social comparison, proposed by **psychologist Leon Festinger,**[2] suggests that people evaluate their own worth and abilities

---

1.   https://www.researchgate.net/figure/Theoretical-approaches-to-jealousy_fig3_328328875

2.   https://link.springer.com/referenceworkentry/10.1007/
978-94-007-0753-5_2740#_853ae90f0351324bd73ea615e6487517__4c761f170e016836ff
84498202b99827__853ae90f0351324bd73ea615e6487517_text_43ec3e5dee6e706af7766
fffea512721_Social_0bcef9c45bd8a48eda1b26eb0c61c869_20comparison_0bcef9c45bd8
a48eda1b26eb0c61c869_20theory_0bcef9c45bd8a48eda1b26eb0c61c869_20was_0bcef9c
45bd8a48eda1b26eb0c61c869_20first_c0cb5f0fcf239ab3d9c1fcd31fff1efc_their_0bcef9c
45bd8a48eda1b26eb0c61c869_20own_0bcef9c45bd8a48eda1b26eb0c61c869_20opinion

by comparing themselves to others. This comparison can lead to feelings of jealousy and envy. This happens when people begin to perceive themselves as less successful or fortunate.

Historical and Cultural Perspectives on Jealousy and Envy

There are also historical and cultural undertones to the human emotions of jealousy and envy.

Jealousy and envy have been pervasive throughout history and across cultures. They have contributed to the shaping of social dynamics, literature, and art.

Mythology and Literature

Ancient myths and literary works are replete with tales of jealousy and envy. For example, the Greek myth of Hera's jealousy over Zeus's infidelities and Shakespeare's portrayal of envy in characters like Iago in "Othello," demonstrates how these emotions can quickly become powerful and destructive forces.

Cultural Variations

Different cultures have varying attitudes towards jealousy and envy. In some cultures, these emotions are openly acknowledged and discussed, while in others, they are seen as taboo and repressed. Understanding these cultural differences can provide some insight into how jealousy and envy are expressed and managed in different societies.

Religious Views

Many religions address jealousy and envy, often viewing them as negative emotions to be overcome. For instance, in Christianity, envy is one of the Seven Deadly Sins. Buddhism encourages detachment and contentment to counteract these dark feelings.

Are Jealousy, Envy and Hatred Related?

Jealousy, envy, and hatred are indeed related emotions, though they have distinct characteristics and may sometimes arise from varying circumstances.

---

s_0bcef9c45bd8a48eda1b26eb0c61c869_20and_0bcef9c45bd8a48eda1b26eb0c61c869_2 0abilities.

While jealousy, envy, and hatred are distinct emotions, they share common roots in feelings of insecurity, inadequacy, and social comparison.

Jealousy often involves a fear of losing something valuable, while envy is driven by a desire for what someone else possesses.

Both can lead to hatred if the other two negative emotions of jealousy and envy are intense and unresolved.

Thus, your understanding of these emotions can help you manage them effectively so that you can cultivate healthier relationships and also achieve personal growth in your unique way.

Let's take a closer look at how jealousy, envy and hatred are interrelated.

Jealousy

We've already identified jealousy as a complex emotion that typically arises when someone perceives a threat to a valued relationship or possession. In many cases, jealousy involves feelings of insecurity, fear, and anxiety.

2 Common Scenarios Involving Jealousy

- A person feels jealous when their romantic partner pays attention to someone else.

- Sibling rivalry often involves jealousy when one child perceives the other as receiving more attention or resources from parents.

2 Characteristics of Jealousy

- Jealousy involves a triadic relationship: the jealous person, the person they are attached to, and a third party perceived as a threat.

- It is often driven by the fear of loss.

Envy

Again, we observed early on that envy is the feeling of wanting what someone else has. It involves a longing for another person's qualities, achievements, or possessions.

2 Common Scenarios Involving Envy

- A person envies a colleague's promotion or success.

- Someone might envy a friend's or neighbour's talent, wealth, or lifestyle.

2 Characteristics of Envy

- Envy involves a dyadic (two-person) relationship: the envious person and the envied person.

- It is driven by the desire for something that one lacks but perceives another as possessing.

Hatred

The third emotion that tends to often bring the above emotions of envy and jealousy together is hatred. We've already defined hatred so here is a reminder.

Hatred is an intense feeling of dislike or animosity toward someone or something. It often involves a desire to harm or see harm come to the object of hatred.

Quite often, envy or jealousy ultimately leads to hatred.

4. Common Scenarios Involving Hatred

- A person might feel hatred towards someone who has wronged them significantly.

- When someone is unhappy that they are not doing so well as compared to a neighbour, workplace colleague or a sibling, it can lead to feelings of hatred.

- A person will harbour feelings of hatred towards someone they believe is undermining their love relationship with a third party.

- Hatred can arise from deeply ingrained prejudices or long-standing conflicts.

2 Characteristics of Hatred

- Hatred can be directed towards individuals, groups, or abstract concepts (e.g., hatred of injustice).

- It often involves a desire for revenge or destruction.

Connecting Jealousy, Envy and Hatred

Let's see the various ways in which jealousy, envy and hatred are interconnected.

1. Jealousy and Envy

- Both jealousy and envy involve social comparisons and negative emotions about oneself relative to others.

- Jealousy can often include elements of envy. For example, a person may be jealous of their partner's new friend because they envy the attention their partner is giving to this friend.

2. Envy and Hatred

Envy can be a source of inspiration that leads to self-improvement. This is when the envious individual views the envied person's accomplishments or position as a motivating call to action.

Unfortunately, the problem with envy is that it can sometimes evolve into hatred. When envy is particularly intense or prolonged, it can lead to deep resentment and eventually to hatred toward the person who is perceived as having what the envious person lacks.

Also, since envy involves wanting what someone else has, when one feels they cannot obtain it, this frustration can turn into destructive hatred.

3. Jealousy and Hatred

Jealousy can also turn into hatred over time. This can easily happen if the perceived threat is persistent and causes significant distress.

If someone feels constantly insecure or threatened by your actions (real or perceived), these feelings can morph into hatred.

- For example, a person might start to hate a rival who consistently outshines them or threatens their important relationships.

Summary of the Key Differences between Jealousy and Envy

Please, note the basic difference between jealousy and envy as summarized below.

Jealousy: It is often about a relationship involving three parties and relates to the fear of losing something such as attention or someone's love.

Envy: It involves two parties, a desire for something someone else has namely possessions, qualities, and achievements.

The next chapter will discuss the specific behavioural and emotional indicators that can help you identify jealousy and envy both in yourself and others.

CONTINUE TO CHAPTER 2: HOW TO SPOT JEALOUSY AND ENVY FROM AFAR

Chapter 2: How to Spot Jealousy and Envy from Afar

We have moved away from the introductory part. In this second chapter, we will explore the various ways to identify both jealousy and envy either in ourselves or in others we relate to. We shall also discuss the reasons why some people tend to attract so many haters and envious people.

Section 1: Telltale Signs of Envy and Jealousy

It is important for you to develop the skills needed to spot the behavioural and emotional signs of jealousy and envy both in yourself and those around you. This way, it becomes easier to take proactive steps to address these feelings. Your constructive response will help foster healthier relationships and a more positive outlook on life.

Here are the areas we will discuss concerning the emotions of jealousy and envy in this chapter.

- Behavioural indicators

- Emotional responses and self-reflection

- Case studies and real-life examples

Behavioural Indicators of Envy and Jealousy

Your ability to quickly spot the signs of envy and jealousy in both yourself and others is crucial for addressing and managing these emotions. Here are some key behavioural indicators to look out for.

1. Subtle Digs and Backhanded Compliments

- Be on the lookout for remarks that seem like compliments but carry an underlying tone of sarcasm or criticism.

- Example: "You're really good at this for someone with no formal training."

2. Avoidance and Exclusion

- When you deliberately exclude someone (or you are deliberately excluded) from social gatherings, conversations, or decision-making processes.

- Example: Anytime a successful colleague is overlooked or not invited to a team lunch or social event, it is a sign that jealousy or envy might be behind the decision.

3. Excessive Comparison

- A habit of constantly comparing yourself to others, leading to feelings of inadequacy or superiority.

- Example: Regularly checking a peer's social media to compare achievements and lifestyle is a possible pointer to a feeling of jealousy or envy.

4. Sabotage and Other Undermining Tactics

- Intentional actions to hinder or undermine someone's success or reputation.

- Example: Jealousy and envy can lead to hurtful actions against others such as spreading rumours, backbiting, character assassination, withholding vital information or providing misleading information to create obstacles.

5. Overly Competitive Behaviour

- Displaying an intense need to outdo others, even in trivial matters.

- Example: Jealous and envious people quickly turn friendly competitions into serious rivalries. They are always trying to one-up the target of their envy and jealousy.

6. Passive-Aggressive Actions

- Indirect expressions of hostility, such as silent treatment, insinuations, procrastination, or making excuses.

- Example: This may come in the form of deliberately delaying responses to messages or failing to complete tasks that will benefit others.

7. Frequent Criticism and Judgment

- Regularly pointing out flaws or shortcomings in others' achievements or possessions.

- Example: Criticizing a friend's new purchase or downplaying someone's professional success.

Emotional Responses and Self-Reflection

Emotions play a significant role in identifying jealousy and envy. Each time you exhibit these emotional responses, you can employ self-reflection to uncover any feelings of jealousy and envy you may be harbouring.

1. Resentment and Bitterness

- Feeling resentful or bitter about someone else's success or happiness.

- Self-Reflection: Ask yourself if you feel joy for others' achievements or if it triggers negative emotions.

2. Anxiety and Insecurity

- Experiencing anxiety or insecurity when comparing yourself to others.

- Self-Reflection: Consider if you often worry about how you measure up to peers or feel threatened by their success.

3. Anger and Frustration

- Feeling angry or frustrated when others achieve what you desire.

- Self-Reflection: Reflect on whether your anger is justified or rooted in jealousy.

4. Desire for Possession

- Intense longing for someone else's possessions, qualities, or achievements.

- Self-Reflection: Identify if you frequently wish for what others have instead of appreciating your own assets.

5. Sense of Injustice

- Believing that others don't deserve their success or that life is unfair.

- Self-Reflection: Evaluate if you often think others' achievements are undeserved and question the fairness of situations.

Further Illustrations: Case Studies and Real-Life Examples

The following real-life examples and case studies provide deeper insights to guide you in recognizing jealousy and envy when you see or experience one. The outcomes show you how to proactively respond in such situations to heal your relationships from jealousy, envy and hatred.

1. Case Study: The Envious Colleague

- Scenario: Jane and Sheila work in the same department. Jane gets a promotion, and Sheila starts making passive-aggressive comments about Jane's work quality.

- Behavioural Indicators: Lisa's subtle digs, avoidance of Jane, and increased competitiveness.

- Emotional Response: Lisa feels insecure about her own career progression and resents Jane's success.

- Outcome: Jane confronts Lisa, leading to a candid discussion about Lisa's feelings and their impact on the workplace environment.

2. Case Study: The Jealous Friend

- Scenario: Mark notices his friend Tom becoming distant and critical after Mark starts dating someone new.

- Behavioural Indicators: Tom's exclusion of Mark from social plans and frequent criticism of Mark's relationship.

- Emotional Response: Tom feels threatened by the potential loss of Mark's attention and friendship.

- Outcome: Mark addresses the issue directly with Tom, reassuring him of their friendship's importance.

3. Case Study: Social Media Envy

- Scenario: Evelyn spends hours scrolling through Instagram, feeling increasingly inadequate compared to her peers' seemingly perfect lives.

- Behavioral Indicators: Excessive comparison and frequent criticism of her own achievements.

- Emotional Response: Evelyn experiences anxiety, resentment, and a desire for a lifestyle similar to those she follows online.

- Outcome: Evelyn reduces her social media usage and focuses on her offline personal growth efforts and daily expressions of gratitude.

Congratulations. You have successfully covered the key areas you need to tackle to know and acknowledge envy and jealousy each time you encounter them. It's time for us to continue to the next section in this chapter: Why You Attract Haters and Envious People. This segment will explore the reasons behind why individuals attract envy and hatred and how to manage these situations.

Section 2: Reasons Why You Attract Haters and Envious People

We will begin this section with an overview of the 12 common reasons why you may be attracting envy, jealousy and hatred. This will be followed by an explanation of three groups of factors that tend to trigger these emotions.

- 12 Common reasons people attract haters
- Success and visibility
- Personal traits and achievements
- Environmental and social factors

12 Common Reasons We Attract Haters and Envious People

You likely attract haters because you are becoming more successful, too self-assured for their liking, or you appear happy and contented. There are several other reasons why some of us attract haters and envious people in our lives.

Usually, it isn't just that your detractors despise you but that they actively look for ways to make life difficult for you.

We all know too many real-life stories of people taking other people's lives due to the intense hatred they harbour in their hearts for their victims.

Thank goodness you and I haven't reached that stage yet. While there is life, there is always hope.

So why do some individuals seem to attract more than their fair share of haters?

In this chapter, we'll explore some key reasons behind this phenomenon. We will shed light on the psychology behind it, with practical examples.

So if you've been looking to understand why you attract haters and jealous people in your life while you haven't done anything to harm them, continue reading and you will find out why.

1. Your Success and Achievement

Haters impatiently watch you to see when you will fail because you seem to be achieving too much success in your endeavours.

For example, when you achieve remarkable success, such as starting a thriving business, jealousy can arise among your peers or neighbours who may not have reached the same level of accomplishment.

2. You're Confident and Self-Assured

Listen to me. You're attracting haters probably because you simply can't help appearing to be in full control of your circumstances.

Some people hate that. This is the unfortunate truth about human nature you and I must learn to live with.

Anyone who exudes confidence and self-assuredness can unknowingly intimidate others who are still struggling with their self-esteem issues.

So your 'annoying' show of bravado could be what is triggering feelings of envy towards you.

3. Your Unique Individuality

You may attract haters just because you are different.

We live in a world where most people take conformity to be a virtue and individuality to be a vice.

Too many people have a herd mentality. And they expect everyone to fall in line without question.

For that matter, if you are an unconventional individual who marches to the beat of your own drum you may face criticism and envy from those who conform to every societal norm.

4. You're Visibly Happy and Satisfied

Someone may hate the very sight of you just because you always look happy and vibrant.

This is more so if they have tried everything to make sure that you go under but see their efforts come to nothing.

It is an unfortunate fact of life that when someone appears genuinely happy and content in their life, it can stir envy in others who may be struggling with their own happiness.

5. You've Achieved Remarkable Personal Growth

Get ready to attract haters and envious people when your life keeps improving despite the challenges you face.

The envy may get vicious when all others around you are crumbling under similar pressures of life.

For example, a commitment to personal growth, like getting in shape or learning a new skill, may elicit envy from those who haven't embarked on such journeys.

6. You Fearlessly Express Your Views

Do you love to say it as it is? Then do not be surprised when people who cannot cope with your frankness despise you.

Quite often, speaking out on controversial topics or expressing unique opinions can lead to criticism from those who prefer to keep their views hidden.

7. You've Built A Strong Support Network

Among the surprising reasons you may attract haters is that some people feel you have too many children, siblings or friends compared to theirs.

In other words, people with robust support networks of friends and family may trigger envy in those who lack such a circle of support.

8. Your Amazing Charisma and Magnetism

It has been proven that individuals with magnetic personalities who easily attract others may face resentment from those who struggle to connect with people.

Do you have an extraordinary magnetic personality? Maybe you naturally have something about you that draws a lot of admirers.

Know from today that people will hate your guts simply because they feel you are too approachable.

9. You're Experiencing Financial Prosperity

Material wealth and financial success can attract envy.

A visible sign of your financial success could be one of the key reasons you attract haters and jealousy.

There are many instances where people turn against their friends and family after comparing their financial situations to theirs and realizing that those loved ones are more affluent.

10. Your Unwavering Resilience

Do you jump back on your feet like a cat each time you fall in life? Then don't be surprised if you see your network of vicious haters expanding.

People hate it when they 'prayed' for your downfall and succeeded only to see you rise from the ashes stronger and happier.

Here is another sad fact of life:

Individuals who bounce back from adversity with resilience and determination may attract haters who find it challenging to do the same.

11. Haters Don't Know the Real You

Quite often, people hate others out of ignorance. They may claim to know you so well that they have every reason to despise you. But the truth remains that they hardly know who you truly are.

We live in a world where some individuals, for reasons best known to them, go around actively working to tarnish the image of others.

Maybe your haters are some of those gullible people who are too willing to believe any one-sided negative report they hear about others without asking the necessary questions.

Know that you are not alone if people dislike you based on hearsay and wild personal assumptions.

Perhaps if they drew closer to learn your true personal story and heard all the facts about you, they wouldn't hate you that much.

12. Haters Love to Hate

Finally, sometimes you may feel so hated that you begin to think you're the only person in the world facing so much hatred. But that is not true.

Even the haters have their fair share of haters.

The simple truth is that, for some reason, human beings love to hate.

While there may be genuine reasons for this in some cases, in most instances, people will hate you just because they feel the need to hate someone. It's sad but true.

I personally have had situations where people desperately look for silly, unfounded reasons to hate me.

This uncalled-for kind of hatred suddenly disappears when the same haters need something from you only to resurface when the need is no more. Funny but true.

Let's now look at the bigger picture. We will focus on three major factors that may be responsible for your being hated by somebody or a certain group of people.

Your Success and Visibility

One of the primary reasons people attract haters and envious individuals is their success and visibility. When someone achieves a level of success that others aspire to, it often triggers feelings of inadequacy and jealousy in those who feel they cannot attain the same level of achievement.

Let's break it down.

1. Professional Success

- Promotions, awards, and recognition in the workplace can attract envy.

- Example: A colleague who receives a significant promotion may find that peers become distant or critical.

2. Personal Accomplishments

- Achievements such as completing a degree, publishing a book, or winning a competition can be sources of envy.

- Example: Completing a marathon or a significant personal project might lead others to downplay your efforts. This reaction is a sign of envy.

3. Public Recognition

- When you're in the public eye, whether through social media, public speaking, or media appearances, it can make you a target for envy and hatred.

- Example: An influencer with a large following may receive negative comments or personal attacks from envious viewers.

Your Personal Traits and Achievements

Certain personal traits and achievements can also attract envy. These can include qualities or accomplishments that others admire but may feel they lack or cannot achieve.

Here are some well-known examples of personal attributes that others find offensive and irritating – all out of envy.

1. Charisma and Confidence

- Natural charisma and confidence can make others feel insecure or inadequate.

- Example: A charismatic leader in a social group may inadvertently make others feel overshadowed.

2. Physical Appearance

- Attractiveness or a well-maintained physical appearance can be a source of envy.

- Example: Receiving compliments on your looks might provoke jealous remarks from others.

3. Intellectual and Creative Abilities

- Your exceptional intelligence or creativity can lead to envy from those who wish they possessed similar talents.

- Example: A talented artist or musician may face jealousy from peers who struggle to achieve the same level of skill.

4. Lifestyle and Possessions

- When you nurture and display a desirable lifestyle, including financial stability, a beautiful home, or luxury items, can attract envy.

- Example: Owning a new car or going on an exotic vacation might lead to envious comments or resentment from others.

Environmental and Social Factors

The environment and social circles we inhabit often play a significant role in attracting envy and haters to ourselves. Let's look at a few scenarios.

1. Competitive Environments

- High-pressure environments such as competitive workplaces or academic institutions tend to be fertile grounds for feelings of envy and jealousy.

- Example: In a competitive office setting, colleagues may view each other's success as a threat to their own advancement.

2. Social Circles

- The dynamics within social groups such as sporting clubs, religious organizations or churches and unions can foster envy, especially if there is a perceived hierarchy of success or popularity.

- Example: In a group of friends, if one person consistently achieves more success or receives more attention, it can lead to jealousy among the others.

3. Cultural and Societal Expectations

- Societal norms, values and cultural expectations can influence how success and achievement are perceived, often leading to envy.

- Example: In cultures that place a high value on material success, individuals who attain wealth may be envied by those who struggle financially.

The same applies to settings where a high premium is placed on marriage and childbearing. Those who, for some reason, are unable to live up to those expectations tend to envy their 'successful' peers.

CONTINUE TO CHAPTER 3.

Chapter 3: The Impact of Jealousy and Envy

Welcome to Chapter 3. In this segment, we will explore the consequences of jealousy and envy. We will continue to use these terms interchangeably as they tend to create the same effects on both the one who harbours them and their victims.

By the time you finish going through the following sections, you will be in a better position to appreciate the need to decisively deal with these emotions wherever and whenever you experience them.

- The Dangers Haters Pose to Your Aspirations and Goals
- Jealousy in Personal Relationships
- Envy in the Workplace
- Envy and Jealousy in Social Media and Digital Spaces

Section 1: The Dangers Haters Pose to Your Aspirations and Goals

It is now clear that jealousy and envy are two major sources of the intense hatred a lot of people harbour against their partners, friends, neighbours and workplace colleagues.

A disturbing fact is that this kind of hatred, if not checked can cause mental, emotional and physical harm to the parties involved. Let's explore these dangers and how they can potentially, hurt your aspirations in building a better life.

- Sabotage and undermining efforts
- Psychological impacts and stress
- Examples from various fields (career, personal projects, etc.

Sabotage and Undermining Efforts

One of the most direct ways people who hate you out of jealousy or envy can impact your aspirations and goals is through sabotage and undermining efforts. This can take various forms, from subtle undermining comments to more overt actions aimed at obstructing your progress.

1. Subtle Sabotage

- Negative comments and pessimistic attitudes from a hater can erode your confidence.

- Example: A colleague consistently questions your ideas during meetings, making you doubt your competence.

2. Direct Undermining

- Haters love to indulge in actions that directly interfere with your work or projects.

- Example: Someone intentionally withholds important information that you need to complete a project on time.

3. Social Sabotage

- Someone who hates you out of jealousy or envy will stop at nothing to damage your reputation or relationships within your professional or social circles.

This is a sad reality I personally experienced when I moved to a neighbourhood in the town I currently live in. It is a move I've always regretted even up to this day.

- Example: Spreading rumours, lies and half-truths about your personal life to tarnish your image.

Psychological Impacts and Stress

The psychological impacts of dealing with haters and envious individuals can be profound.

Persistent exposure to negativity can lead to stress, anxiety, and a decrease in overall well-being.

1. Increased Stress Levels

- Constantly having to deal with negative individuals can increase stress and affect your mental health.

- Example: Feeling anxious or stressed about attending work or social events where you might encounter negative individuals.

2. Erosion of Self-Confidence

- Persistent destructive criticism and name-calling from haters can erode your self-confidence and self-esteem.

- Example: Doubting your abilities or decisions because of constant criticism from others.

3. Mental Fatigue

- The emotional toll of managing envy and hate can lead to mental exhaustion and burnout.

- Example: You can feel mentally drained after interacting with negative people. This can undermine your productivity and focus.

Examples from Various Fields

Envy and jealousy can affect aspirations and goals across different fields. Some of these are career, personal projects, and social endeavours.

1. Career and Professional Life

- In the workplace, jealousy can manifest in competitive behaviour, backstabbing, and lack of cooperation.

- Example: An envious team member deliberately excludes you from important meetings or projects to hinder your progress.

2. Personal Projects and Hobbies

- Jealousy and envy can stifle creativity and passion for personal projects and hobbies.

- Example: Deliberately concocted negative feedback from envious peers discourages you from pursuing your passion project.

3. Social and Community Involvement

- Deliberate hateful acts and utterances from envious individuals can disrupt your involvement in social and community activities, creating tension and conflict.

- Example: A community member spreading false information about your motives or actions to discredit your efforts and tarnish your image.

This is a reality I've had to live with for many years when I relocated to a new place I thought would have otherwise improved my social life.

Ways to Overcome Sabotage and Psychological Impacts

To protect our aspirations and goals from the dangers posed by haters and envious individuals, we must consciously develop strategies for resilience and perseverance.

1. Strengthen Your Support Network

- Surround yourself with supportive, positive individuals who encourage and uplift you.

- Example: Build a network of mentors, friends, and colleagues who provide constructive feedback and emotional support.

2. Practice Self-Affirmation

- Regularly engage in self-affirmation exercises to boost your confidence and self-esteem.

- Example: Start each day with positive affirmations about your abilities and achievements.

3. Focus on Personal Growth

- Concentrate on your personal and professional development, setting clear goals and tracking progress.

- Example: Enrol in courses, attend workshops, or seek new challenges that align with your aspirations.

4. Communicate Openly and Assertively

- Address negative behaviour directly and assertively. Make sure to set clear boundaries.

- Example: Have a candid conversation with a colleague who undermines you. Show them how their behaviour is negatively affecting you and what changes you expect.

5. Document and Report

- In professional settings, document instances of sabotage and report them to relevant authorities if necessary.

- Example: Keep a record of emails, messages, or actions that demonstrate sabotage, and present them to HR or a supervisor.

6. Seek Professional Help

- If the psychological impacts of dealing with haters become overwhelming, seek help from a mental health professional.

- Example: Therapy or counselling can provide strategies for coping with stress, and anxiety and maintaining mental health.

Turning Negativity into Motivation

Instead of letting haters and envious individuals derail your aspirations, use their negativity as motivation to fuel your progress. I consider this to be one of the best ways to put our haters to shame.

1. Transform Criticism into Constructive Feedback

- View negative comments as opportunities to improve and grow.

- Example: Analyse valid points in criticism and use them to refine your skills and approach.

2. Use Envy as a Benchmark for Success

- Recognize that envy often indicates you are achieving something significant.

- Example: Let the negativity coming from those who envy you motivate you to continue striving for excellence and achieving your goals.

3. Stay Focused on Your Vision

- Maintain a clear focus on your long-term vision and goals, regardless of external negativity.

- Example: Create a vision board or a detailed plan that keeps you oriented towards your objectives. It will keep reminding you why you started.

It's time to look at something interesting in another section: Jealousy in Personal Relationships. We are about to explore how jealousy manifests in different types of personal relationships.

Section 2: Jealousy in Personal Relationships

- Signs of jealousy in friendships, family, and romantic relationships
    - The impact on trust and communication
    - Case studies and personal stories
    Signs of Jealousy in Friendships
    Jealousy in friendships can manifest in subtle and overt ways. Whenever this happens, it undermines trust and harmony. Here are some common pointers to jealousy in friendships.

1. Competitive Behaviour

- Friends who feel jealous may engage in competitive behaviour. Such friends will engage in all manner of ploys to outdo or overshadow you.

- Example: If you share an achievement, such as a job promotion or personal milestone, a jealous friend might immediately respond with their own accomplishments. Such a person will begin to act in ways that are meant to take you out of the spotlight and shift the focus onto themselves.

2. Withholding Support

- A jealous friend might withhold support or downplay your successes to diminish their impact.

- Example: Instead of congratulating you on a significant achievement, they might make dismissive comments like, "That's nice, but it's not that big of a deal."

3. Gossip and Rumour-Spreading

- A jealous friend might spread rumours or gossip about you to tarnish your reputation or create conflict within your social circle.

- Example: Sharing private or misleading information about your personal life with others to damage your image.

4. Exclusion and Isolation

- A jealous or envious friend will intentionally exclude you from social events or gatherings to make you feel left out and inferior.

- Example: They plan key activities without inviting you. Sometimes, they behave in ways that make you feel like an outsider in your own group of friends.

Signs of Jealousy in Family Relationships

Family relationships can be particularly challenging when jealousy is involved, as these bonds are often deep-rooted and complex.

1. Sibling Rivalry

- Jealousy among siblings can lead to rivalry, competition, and tension within the family.

- Example: One sibling using any conceivable means to get the best results, not to excel, but with the sole purpose of outperforming another in academics, sports, or career achievements to gain parental approval.

There are situations where a brother or sister will flare up in anger when it appears a particular sibling is getting too much attention, affection or favours, in their opinion.

2. Parental Jealousy

- Parents can sometimes feel jealous of their children's accomplishments, especially if they feel their own lives are lacking.

- Example: A parent feeling threatened by their child's success and responding with critical or dismissive remarks instead of pride and support.

3. Comparative Comments

- Family members making frequent comparisons between you and other relatives, highlighting your perceived shortcomings.

- Example: An aunt or uncle constantly comparing your achievements to those of your cousins, making you feel inadequate or undervalued. I personally saw too much of this, growing up.

4. Attempts to Undermine Relationships

- Jealous family members may attempt to undermine your relationships with other family members to create discord.

- Example: Spreading false information about those we envy or sowing seeds of doubt about our intentions and actions to other relatives.

Signs of Jealousy in Romantic Relationships

Jealousy in romantic relationships can be particularly damaging. Quite often, it results in trust issues and emotional distress.

The signs of jealousy and envy in romantic relationships are many. Here are a few.

1. Possessiveness and Control

- A jealous partner may exhibit possessive and controlling behaviour. Such an individual will go to every length to monitor your actions and restrict your interactions with others.

- Example: Frequently checking your phone, demanding to know your whereabouts, or limiting your social interactions to maintain control.

I know relationships where out of jealousy, one partner will turn into a control freak. They take deliberate steps to cut off anyone they consider a threat.

One unfortunate tactic insecure jealous partners use is to make sure the other partner fails at every effort aimed at achieving personal growth. This way, not only will the partner lack the means to help others they care about but will also end up becoming financially dependent on them.

It's like they literally sit tight on your dreams and progress to help them take care of their own insecurities and inadequacies in the relationship.

2. Misplaced Accusations and Suspicion

- Unfounded accusations and constant suspicion of infidelity or dishonesty can erode trust and intimacy.

- Example: Accusing you of cheating without any evidence or constantly questioning your loyalty and fidelity.

3. Emotional Manipulation

- A jealous romantic partner may use guilt, blame, or emotional blackmail to manipulate your behaviour and make you feel responsible for their jealousy.

- Example: Saying things like, "If you really loved me, you wouldn't need to spend time with anyone else," to make you feel guilty for having a social life.

Also, a jealous partner who has morphed into a control freak will feign near-death sickness just to make their victim capitulate to their whims and caprices.

4. Isolation from Friends and Family

- Some jealous partners will stop at nothing to cut you from your support network just to maintain their seeming power and control.

- Example: Your spouse discourages, forbids or acts in ways that undermine your ability to spend time with friends and family. Their goal is to make you more reliant on them for emotional support.

The Impact of Jealousy on Trust and Communication

Jealousy can severely impact trust and communication in personal relationships, leading to long-term damage if not addressed.

1. Erosion of Trust

- Persistent jealousy and suspicion can erode the foundation of trust, making it difficult to maintain a healthy relationship.

- Example: Constantly doubting each other's intentions and actions, leading to a cycle of distrust and resentment.

2. Breakdown in Communication

- Jealousy can hinder open and honest communication. This can lead to misunderstandings and conflict.

- Example: The victim begins to avoid important conversations or hides their true feelings out of fear of triggering jealousy, anger or even the onset of an imaginary near-death medical condition in the jealous partner.

3. Increased Conflict and Tension

- Unresolved jealousy can lead to frequent arguments and tension, straining the relationship.

- Example: Small disagreements escalate into major conflicts due to underlying jealousy and insecurity.

4. Emotional Distance

- Over time, jealousy can create emotional distance, reducing intimacy and connection.

- Example: A partner withdraws emotionally to protect themselves from the pain caused by jealousy and suspicion in the other party.

Case Studies and Personal Stories

Let's examine some real-life examples that will provide valuable insights into how jealousy manifests and its devastating consequences for personal relationships.

1. Case Study: Jealousy in Friendship

- Scenario: Joyce and Stephanie have been friends since college. When Joyce starts a successful business, Stephanie begins making sarcastic comments and withdrawing from their friendship.

- Behavioural Indicators: Stephanie's competitive remarks, lack of support, and exclusion from social events.

- Emotional Impact: Joyce feels hurt and confused by Stephanie's behaviour, leading to tension and a widening distance between them.

- Action and Outcome: After a candid conversation, Stephanie admits her jealousy. This paves the way for them to work on rebuilding trust and support in their friendship.

2. Case Study: Family Jealousy

- Scenario: Abdul's younger brother, Ahmed, receives more praise and attention from their parents due to his academic achievements. Abdul feels jealous and starts avoiding family gatherings.

- Behavioral Indicators: Abdul's withdrawal, open hostility, critical comments about Ahmed, and increased tension at family events.

- Emotional Impact: Abdul's feelings of inadequacy and resentment towards Ahmed and their parents.

- Action and Outcome: Family therapy helps address the underlying issues. The result is an improvement in communication and lessening of jealousy within the family.

3. Case Study: Romantic Jealousy

- Scenario: Chika and Mike have been dating for two years. Mike becomes increasingly jealous and possessive, frequently accusing Chika of cheating without evidence.

- Behavioral Indicators: Mike's possessiveness, accusations, and attempts to isolate Chika from her friends.

- Emotional Impact: Chika feels trapped and anxious, leading to a decline in the relationship's quality.

- Action and Outcome: Chika sets boundaries and insists on couples counselling. Mike agrees to work on his jealousy, and their relationship gradually improves.

Strategies for Managing Jealousy in Personal Relationships

To effectively manage jealousy in any personal relationship, self-awareness, communication, and proactive strategies are required. These will build trust and understanding.

1. Develop Self-Awareness

- Recognize and acknowledge feelings of jealousy when they arise.

- Example: Reflect on the triggers and underlying insecurities that contribute to your jealousy.

2. Communicate Openly

- Have honest conversations about your feelings and concerns with the people involved.

- Example: Share your feelings of jealousy with your friend, family member, or partner in a non-confrontational manner.

3. Set Healthy Boundaries

- Establish clear boundaries to protect your emotional well-being.

- Example: Discuss and agree on boundaries regarding social interactions, personal space, and privacy.

4. Practice Empathy and Understanding

- Try to understand the perspective and feelings of others involved.

- Example: Consider how your actions or achievements might unintentionally impact others. Proactively address their feelings with humility and empathy.

5. Focus on Personal Growth

- Work on building self-confidence and addressing insecurities that fuel jealousy.

- Example: Engage in activities that boost self-esteem and foster personal development.

6. Seek Professional Help

- Consider therapy or counselling to address deep-seated jealousy and its impact on relationships.

- Example: Individual or couples therapy can provide strategies and support for managing jealousy effectively.

How to Promote Healthy Relationships

To create and nurture healthy relationships demands continuous effort, communication, and mutual respect. Here are some action points to help you work towards building healthy relationships.

1. Celebrate Each Other's Successes

- Genuinely celebrate and support each other's achievements and milestones.

- Example: Congratulate and express pride in a friend's or partner's accomplishments.

2. Cultivate Trust and Transparency

- Build trust through honesty, reliability, and openness.

- Example: Share your thoughts and feelings openly. Do not forget to follow through on your commitments and promises.

3. Maintain a Positive Outlook on Life

- Focus on the positive aspects of your relationships and work on resolving conflicts constructively.

- Example: Practice gratitude and appreciation for the people in your life. Genuinely highlight their positive qualities and contributions.

4. Invest in Quality Time Together

- Spend meaningful time together to strengthen your bond.

- Example: Plan regular activities, outings, or quality time that promotes closeness and understanding.

Congratulations. You've just finished studying a critical segment of this book. You've learnt how to recognize the signs of jealousy in your relationships.

I believe that when you actively implement the recommended strategies to manage this emotion, you will contribute significantly to nurturing healthier, more supportive, and fulfilling connections with friends, family, and romantic partners.

Before us is the next section of this chapter: Envy in the Workplace. This segment will explore professional envy, jealousy and competition, and their effects on teamwork and productivity.

Section 3: Envy in the Workplace

- Professional jealousy, envy and competition
    - Effects on teamwork and productivity
    - Strategies for navigating workplace envy
    Prevalence of Professional Jealousy, Envy and Competition

Professional envy is common in competitive workplaces where individuals strive for recognition, promotions, and success. This type of envy can manifest in various ways, affecting team dynamics and individual performance.

Let's consider some well-known cases of professional jealousy, envy and completion in most working environments.

1. Competitiveness Instead of Collaboration

- In highly competitive environments, employees may prioritize personal achievements over team success. This attitude tends to engender feelings of envy and jealousy.

- Example: Colleagues competing for the same promotion might engage in one-upmanship. They may withhold information or resources that could benefit the team.

2. Recognition and Rewards

- Unequal recognition and rewards can trigger envy among employees who feel undervalued or overlooked.

- Example: If one employee consistently receives praise and bonuses while others' contributions go unnoticed, envy and resentment can arise.

3. Comparison of Skills and Achievements

- Employees frequently compare their skills, achievements, and career progression to their peers, leading to feelings of inadequacy and envy.

- Example: A staff member who observes a colleague's rapid advancement while they feel stuck in the same position will begin to feel envious. This can lead to diminished morale and further underachievement.

Effects on Teamwork and Productivity

It is a well-known fact that envy in the workplace creates a toxic work environment. This can have detrimental effects on teamwork, productivity, and overall morale.

Here are some of the most consequential negative effects of a pervading atmosphere of envy in any work environment.

1. Decreased Collaboration

- Envy and jealousy can hinder collaboration as employees become reluctant to share knowledge or support each other.

- Example: An employee who feels envious of a colleague's success might avoid working with them or providing assistance. This will negatively impact team cohesion.

2. Lowered Productivity

- The emotional toll of jealousy can lead to decreased motivation and productivity, as employees focus more on interpersonal conflicts than their work.

- Example: There are numerous situations where envious workers spend time and energy on gossip or undermining others instead of focusing on tasks and goals.

3. Increased Conflict

- Professional envy and jealousy can lead to conflicts, arguments, and tension within the team. This can lead to a disruption in the workflow.

- Example: Disagreements over credit for work or accusations of favouritism can escalate into larger conflicts that affect the entire team.

4. Erosion of Trust

- Envy and jealousy undermine trust among team members. In such an environment, it becomes difficult to build productive working relationships.

- Example: If employees suspect that their colleagues are envious or working against them, it can erode trust and cooperation.

Strategies for Navigating Workplace Envy

To create a positive and productive work environment, it's essential to implement strategies to manage and mitigate envy.

1. Promote Open Communication

- Encourage open and honest communication to address issues of jealousy or envy.

- Example: Regular team meetings where employees can voice their concerns and discuss issues constructively.

2. Promote a Culture of Collaboration

- Create a workplace culture that values collaboration over competition, and emphasizes team achievements over individual triumphs.

- Example: Rewarding team success with group incentives and recognizing collaborative efforts in performance reviews.

3. Recognize and Appreciate All Contributions

- Avoid selective recognition. Ensure that all employees feel valued and recognized for their contributions, regardless of their role.

- Example: Implementing a recognition program that highlights the efforts and achievements of all team members.

4. Provide Opportunities for Professional Development

- Offer training, mentorship, and development opportunities to help employees grow and advance in their careers.

- Example: Regularly providing workshops, courses, and mentorship programs to support career progression.

5. Encourage Self-Reflection and Growth

- Encourage employees to focus on their personal growth and self-improvement rather than comparing themselves to others.

- Example: Providing resources for self-assessment and setting personal development goals.

6. Address and Resolve Conflicts Promptly

- Address conflicts arising from jealousy quickly and fairly to prevent them from escalating.

- Example: Mediating and settling disputes amicably. One way to achieve this is to provide a platform for employees to resolve their differences constructively.

Case Studies and Personal Stories

The following real-life examples provide insights into how professional envy manifests and how it can be managed effectively.

Let's study them one after the other.

1. Case Study: Envy Arising from Promotions

- Scenario: Alicia and Kofi work in the same department. Alicia is promoted to a senior position. This leads to Kofi feeling envious and resentful.

- Behavioural Indicators: Kofi becomes less cooperative. He criticizes Alicia's decisions, and spreads falsehoods about her qualifications.

- Impact: The team's productivity decreases, and tension rises due to Kofi's behaviour.

- Action and Resolution: The manager addresses the issue by discussing Kofi's concerns. He offers him development opportunities. This goes a long way to promote a more collaborative environment.

2. Case Study: Envy in a Creative Team

- Scenario: In a marketing agency, Angela consistently produces high-quality work and receives praise. Her colleague, Fernandez, starts feeling envious and begins to undermine her ideas.

- Behavioural Indicators: Fernandez dismisses Angela's ideas in meetings and takes credit for her contributions.

- Impact: The team's creativity and morale suffer due to the ongoing conflict.

- Resolution: The agency implements regular brainstorming sessions where all ideas are credited to the team. This timely intervention reduces individual competition and increases collaboration within the team.

Long-Term Strategies for a Positive Work Environment

To create a sustainable positive work environment for your staff, you need to pursue an ongoing effort aimed at managing envy. This can promote mutual respect and support.

Here are some recommendations to consider.

1. Implement Fair Policies and Practices

- Develop and enforce fair policies that ensure equal opportunities and transparent processes for recognition and advancement.

- Example: You can draw and implement transparent criteria for promotions and rewards, conduct regular performance reviews, and other feedback mechanisms.

2. Cultivate Emotional Intelligence

- Encourage employees to develop emotional intelligence skills, such as empathy, self-awareness, and conflict resolution.

- Example: Organize workshops and training sessions on emotional intelligence and interpersonal skills.

3. Build a Supportive Leadership Team

- Ensure that leaders and managers set the tone for a positive, supportive work environment.

- Example: Leaders can model collaborative behaviour, provide regular feedback, and support team members' professional growth.

4. Encourage a Healthy Work-Life Balance

- Promote work-life balance to reduce stress and prevent burnout since these can contribute to destructive emotions among staff.

- Example: Flexible work schedules, remote work options, and wellness programs.

5. Regularly Assess and Improve Workplace Culture

- Continuously assess the workplace culture. Make improvements based on employee feedback and their changing needs.

- Example: Managers, CEOs or Directors can conduct employee surveys, hold focus groups, and implement changes based on feedback.

In this chapter, we learnt the importance of recognizing the prevalence and impact of envy in the workplace. We also saw the need to proactively implement strategies to manage it. These will help organizations to create a positive, collaborative, and productive work environment where all employees feel valued and supported.

Our next destination in this chapter is Section 4: Jealousy in Social Media and Digital Spaces. It is another exciting segment where we will explore how the digital age has amplified feelings of envy, jealousy and hate. As usual, get ready to discover some practical strategies for effectively managing these emotions in online interactions.

Section 4: Envy and Jealousy in Social Media and Digital Spaces

The Rise of Envy in the Digital Age

The emergence of social media and digital platforms has significantly amplified feelings of envy and jealousy. The curated nature of online content often portrays idealized versions of life. This has brought about constant comparisons and heightened insecurities.

Let's look at a few instances that end up creating feelings of envy and jealousy.

1. Curated Perfection

- Social media platforms like Instagram, Facebook, and TikTok encourage users to share highlights of their lives. Most users portray faked personas that create an illusion of perfect lives.

- Example: Influencers posting perfectly edited photos of luxurious vacations, impeccable homes, and enviable lifestyles.

2. Instant Comparisons

- The ease of access to others' lives makes it simple to compare oneself to peers, celebrities, and strangers, often unfavourably.

- Example: Scrolling through a feed filled with friends' career achievements, fitness milestones, and happy relationships can trigger feelings of inadequacy and envy.

3. Validation Through Metrics

- Likes, comments, shares, and follower counts have unfortunately become metrics for measuring social validation. These may create a wrong picture and unfounded impressions. The result is widespread feelings of unworthiness or inadequacy among millions of social media users.

- Example: Your social media post that doesn't receive as many likes as expected can lead to feelings of rejection and self-doubt.

4. Highlight Reels vs. Reality

- Social media often shows highlight reels rather than the full reality, leading to distorted perceptions of others' lives.

- Example: Imagine seeing only the positive moments of someone's life. You will feel extremely impressed and devastated at the same time without acknowledging the challenges and personal struggles they face.

Social Media Comparison and Its Effects

Constant comparison on social media can have several detrimental effects on mental health and self-esteem, exacerbating feelings of jealousy and envy.

1. Decreased Self-Esteem

- The habit of comparing yourself to the seemingly perfect lives of others can produce feelings of inadequacy and low self-esteem.

- Example: Feeling less attractive, successful, or happy compared to peers' online portrayals.

2. Increased Anxiety and Depression

- The pressure to keep up with others and the fear of missing out (FOMO) can contribute to anxiety and depression.

- Example: Experiencing anxiety about not being invited to events or not achieving milestones at the same pace as your peers.

3. Social Isolation

- Envy and jealousy can lead to social withdrawal and isolation, as individuals may feel disconnected from their peers.

- Example: Avoiding social interactions due to feelings of inadequacy or resentment towards friends' successes.

4. Negative Body Image

- Exposure to near-perfect idealized body types and beauty standards on social media can negatively impact body image and self-worth.

- Example: Feeling dissatisfied with one's appearance after seeing photoshopped images of influencers and celebrities.

Managing and Mitigating Digital Envy

To fight and overcome the negative effects of social media comparison, you need to adopt certain strategies for managing and mitigating digital envy.

1. Curate Your Feed

- Take control of your social media feed by following accounts that inspire and uplift you. Unfollow any account or page that triggers envy and insecurity.

- Example: Choose to follow accounts that promote body positivity, mental health, and personal growth rather than unrealistic lifestyles.

2. Limit Screen Time

- Set boundaries for social media usage to reduce exposure to envy-inducing content. Spend the saved time to focus on real-life interactions.

- Example: You can start with setting and sticking to screen time limits, taking regular social media breaks, or using apps that track and limit usage.

3. Practice Mindful Consumption

- Be mindful of how social media content affects your emotions and take steps to engage with it healthily.

- Example: Make time to reflect on your feelings after browsing social media sites. Then adjust your habits accordingly.

4. Focus on Gratitude

Yes, once again, an attitude of gratitude can work in your favour.

- Shift your focus from what you lack to what you have by practicing gratitude regularly.

- Example: Keep a gratitude journal to document things you're thankful for. Do not leave out the small ones.

5. Engage in Real-Life Activities

- Balance online interactions with offline activities that bring joy and fulfilment.

- Example: Spend more time with friends and family. You can also pursue hobbies, or engage in physical activities.

6. Avoid Comparisons

- Remind yourself that everyone's journey is unique, and comparisons are often misleading and harmful.

- Example: Consciously reframing thoughts of comparison to focus on your own progress and achievements.

Case Studies and Personal Stories

We will use the following real-life examples to illustrate the impact of social media envy and provide insights into managing these feelings.

1. Case Study: Overcoming Instagram Envy

- Scenario: Kalala spends hours on Instagram, feeling envious of friends who appear to have perfect lives.

- Behavioural Indicators: Kalala keeps comparing his life to others, leading to feelings of envy, inadequacy and low self-esteem.

- Impact: Kalala's mental health suffers, and he begins to withdraw from social interactions.

- Action and Resolution: Kalala decides to unfollow accounts that trigger envy and starts following positive, motivational content. He also sets screen time limits and begins to focus on real-life activities. Over time, his self-esteem and mental health improve significantly.

2. Case Study: Managing Professional Jealousy on LinkedIn

- Scenario: Amina feels envious when she sees colleagues posting about their promotions and achievements on LinkedIn.

- Behavioural Indicators: Amina feels anxious and inadequate, constantly comparing her career progress to others.

- Impact: Amina's productivity and job satisfaction decline due to constant comparisons.

- Action and Resolution: Amina shifts her focus to her own professional development, setting personal career goals and seeking mentorship. She also limits her time on LinkedIn and engages more in professional development activities. She eventually regains confidence and satisfaction in her career.

Long-Term Strategies for Healthy Social Media Use

To ensure a healthy relationship with social media, you must adopt long-term strategies that reduce feelings of envy. Here are some suggestions to consider.

1. Create a Positive Online Environment

- Foster a positive online presence by sharing uplifting content and engaging constructively with others.

- Example: You can post about real personal achievements while expressing gratitude, and supporting others' successes as well.

2. Practice Digital Detoxes

- Regularly take breaks from social media to recharge and focus on offline experiences.

- Example: Designate specific weekends or certain days as social media-free days to reconnect with real-life activities.

3. Seek Professional Guidance

- If social media envy becomes overwhelming, consider seeking help from a mental health professional.

- Example: Therapy or counselling can provide strategies for managing social media-related envy.

4. Encourage Authenticity

- Promote authenticity on social media by sharing genuine, unfiltered moments and encouraging others to do the same.

- Example: Post about both successes and challenges. This helps create a more realistic portrayal of life.

5. Educate Yourself and Others

- Stay informed about the impact of social media on mental health. Go a step further to educate others about healthy social media use.

- Example: Read articles, attend workshops, and discuss the importance of mindful social media consumption with friends and family.

In this segment, I've tried to help you appreciate the rise of envy in the digital age. You've discovered effective strategies that can help you manage it. I trust that you will take action to promote a healthier relationship with social media in ways that improve your overall well-being and happiness and those of others.

Let's move to another interesting aspect of this discussion in Chapter 4: Overcoming Jealousy and Envy. It includes critical strategies like Self-Reflection and Personal Growth. The chapter expands on the strategies for dealing with jealousy in various environments we covered in Chapter 3.

The goal here is to help you identify your own triggers and vulnerabilities so that you can build self-awareness, and develop resilience in a world filled with so much envy, jealousy and hate.

Chapter 4: How to Overcome Jealousy and Envy

In the previous chapter, we uncovered the consequences of jealousy and envy on our lives and those of others. Since these effects of jealousy and envy are generally unhelpful for our well-being and personal growth, what we must be looking for are ways to fight them. In this chapter, therefore, you will learn some effective techniques and approaches to help you overcome jealousy and envy. So whether you feel you, as an individual, are guilty of feeling jealous and envious of others or you have constantly been at the receiving end of these emotions, it's time for you to learn how to deal with them once and for all.

Here are the topics we will discuss in Chapter 4 spanning across the next four sections.
- Self-Reflection and Personal Growth
- Dealing with Envious or Jealous People
- Thriving Amidst Jealousy and Envy
- Forgiveness and Letting Go

Section 1: Self-Reflection and Personal Growth

- Understanding your own triggers and vulnerabilities
    - Building self-awareness and emotional intelligence
    - Techniques for self-improvement and resilience
    Understanding Your Own Triggers and Vulnerabilities

Self-reflection is a crucial step in identifying the root causes of jealousy and envy. Your ability to identify your own triggers and vulnerabilities will help you to develop strategies to manage these emotions effectively.

1. Identify Triggers

- Recognize specific situations, people, or events that tend to trigger any feelings of jealousy and envy in you.

- Example: You may notice that you feel envious when a colleague receives praise for their work or when you see friends posting about their vacations on social media.

2. Understand Underlying Insecurities

- Reflect on the underlying insecurities that contribute to these triggers. These may relate to feelings of inadequacy or fear of missing out.

- Example: You may discover that your envy of a friend's promotion arises from your own insecurity about your career progress.

3. Analyse Past Experiences

- Consider past experiences that may have shaped your current feelings of jealousy and envy.

- Example: Try to reflect on how past failures or criticisms have shaped your worldview and impacted your self-esteem in ways that have led to the feelings of envy and jealousy you experience now.

4. Self-Assessment Tools

- Utilize self-assessment tools, such as journaling or personality tests, to gain deeper insights into your emotions and behaviour patterns.

- Example: You can keep a daily journal to document moments of jealousy. Devote some time to reflect on their causes and effects.

Building Self-Awareness and Emotional Intelligence

You must develop self-awareness and emotional intelligence as you work to control your frequent feelings of jealousy and envy. These skills help you recognize and regulate your emotions.

Here are some suggestions that have proven effective for many people grappling with feelings of jealousy and envy.

1. Practice Mindfulness

- Mindfulness techniques can help you become more aware of your emotions and reactions in the present moment.

- Example: Engage in mindfulness meditation to observe your thoughts and feelings without judgment. This can increase your awareness of a feeling of jealousy when it arises.

2. Develop Emotional Regulation Skills

- Learn techniques to manage and regulate your emotions. You will then reduce the intensity of jealousy and envy inside you.

- Example: Practice deep breathing exercises or use cognitive restructuring to reframe negative thoughts.

3. Enhance Empathy

- When you cultivate a spirit of empathy it can help you understand perspectives that may not be the same as yours. This can also help reduce feelings of jealousy and envy.

- Example: Always try putting yourself in someone else's shoes to understand better their achievements and struggles. This might develop feelings of compassion and admiration in you rather than envy and hatred.

4. Seek Feedback

- Ask for feedback from trusted friends, family, or mentors to gain an external perspective on your behaviour and emotions.

- Example: You can discuss your feelings of jealousy with a mentor who can provide constructive advice and support.

Techniques for Self-Improvement and Resilience

To achieve personal growth and resilience, you must adopt practices that enhance your self-esteem, confidence, and overall well-being.

Let's look at some of the daily practices that you can use to achieve these.

1. Set Personal Goals

- Establish clear, achievable personal goals to focus on your growth and progress rather than comparing yourself to others.

- Example: You might want to set a goal to learn a new skill or complete a certification course within a specific timeframe.

2. Celebrate Small Wins

- Acknowledge and celebrate your achievements, no matter how small, to boost your confidence and self-esteem.

- Example: Rewarding yourself for meeting a milestone or completing a challenging task. This will reinforce a positive self-regard.

3. Engage in Continuous Learning

- Commit to continuous learning and self-improvement to build competence and confidence.

- Example: Read as many books as you can. Attend workshops, or take online courses to develop new skills and knowledge. Remember, the more knowledgeable you feel, the more self-confident you become.

4. Cultivate a Growth Mindset

- Embrace a development mindset. View challenges and failures as opportunities for learning and growth.

- Example: Adopt the perspective that setbacks are temporary and can lead to personal development and resilience.

5. Practice Self-Compassion

- Treat yourself with kindness and understanding, recognizing that everyone, not only you, experiences setbacks and imperfections.

- Example: Repeat self-compassionate statements, such as "It's okay to feel this way" or "I am doing my best."

Personal Stories and Examples

Take time to examine personal stories and examples. Such stories can provide inspiration and practical insights to guide you in your pursuit of self-reflection and personal growth.

Here are some examples to inspire you.

1. Personal Story: Overcoming Professional Jealousy

- Scenario: Anita felt jealous of her colleague, Michael, who consistently received praise and promotions. She realized that her envy stemmed from her own insecurity about her skills and career progression.

- Self-Reflection: Anita identified her triggers and underlying insecurities, acknowledging that she needed to focus on her growth.

- Actions Taken: Anita set personal career goals, sought mentorship, and engaged in professional development courses. She practised mindfulness and self-compassion to manage her jealousy.

- Outcome: Over time, Anita built her confidence and skills. This led to her own career advancements and a healthier relationship with Michael.

2. Personal Story: Managing Social Media Envy

- Scenario: Frank often felt envious when scrolling through social media, seeing friends' travel photos and career achievements. He realized this was affecting his self-esteem and happiness.

- Self-Reflection: Frank identified his triggers and recognized that his envy was linked to a fear of missing out and a desire for validation.

- Actions Taken: Frank curated his social media feed and unfollowed accounts that triggered envy. He began following only inspirational and positive content. He also set screen time limits and engaged in offline activities that brought him joy.

- Outcome: Frank's self-esteem improved, and he felt more content and focused on his own goals. His social media use became a source of inspiration rather than envy.

Creating a Personal Growth Plan

When you draw and implement a structured personal growth plan it can help you stay focused and motivated on your journey of self-improvement. Here are some steps you can follow to achieve the desired outcomes.

1. Define Your Vision

- Outline a clear vision of who you want to become and what you want to achieve.

- Example: Write a personal mission statement that reflects your values, goals, and aspirations.

2. Set Specific Goals

- Establish specific, measurable, achievable, relevant, and time-bound (SMART) goals that align with your vision.

- Example: Try setting a goal to improve your public speaking skills by attending a course and giving a presentation within six months.

3. Create Action Steps

- Break down your goals into actionable steps, detailing the tasks and resources needed to achieve them.

- Example: Listing the steps to complete a certification course, including enrolling, studying, and taking the final exam.

4. Track Your Progress

- Monitor your progress regularly. Adjust your plan as needed to stay on track.

- Example: You can keep a journal or use a goal-tracking app to document your achievements and reflect on your growth.

5. Seek Support and Accountability

- Share your goals with trusted friends, family, or mentors who can provide support and hold you accountable.

- Example: Join a support group or find an accountability partner to occasionally discuss your progress and challenges.

6. Celebrate Milestones

- Celebrate your achievements and milestones along the way to stay motivated and reinforce positive behaviour.

- Example: Reward yourself with a treat or a day off after completing a major milestone or achieving a significant goal.

You've been learning the importance of understanding your triggers and vulnerabilities, and building self-awareness and emotional intelligence. Additionally, you've uncovered strategies you can implement for personal growth and resilience. This is another big step to effectively manage jealousy and envy in your life so you can achieve a more fulfilling life.

Let's proceed now with Section 2 of this chapter: Dealing with Envious and Jealous People. Here, I will provide strategies for identifying and understanding the motives behind others' envy and jealousy, setting boundaries, and how to manage conflicts effectively.

Section 2: Dealing with Envious or Jealous People

Let's face it. Envious and jealous people are everywhere. It is easy for us to think that our current friends, partners, neighbours or workplace colleagues are the only envious people and haters in the world. But wait till you relocate to a new environment. Then you will quickly realize that there is no escaping from the vermin of haters. This is why it is better to confront and deal with envy, jealousy and hate wherever you are now instead of trying to escape from them.

Let's find out some effective ways to start dealing with envious and jealous people here and now.

Identify and Understand The Motives

To effectively deal with envious and jealous people, it's essential to understand their motives and recognize the signs of envy or jealousy in their behaviour. These are the areas we will tackle in this segment.

1. Insecurity and Low Self-Esteem

- Jealousy or envy often stems from an individual's insecurity and low self-esteem. These are common feelings that ultimately result in people feeling threatened by others' success.

- Example: A colleague who frequently criticizes your work may be projecting their own insecurities about their capabilities.

2. Fear of Loss

- The fear of losing something valuable, such as attention, affection, or status, can trigger jealousy.

- Example: A friend who becomes jealous when you spend time with others may fear losing your friendship or attention.

3. Comparison Mindset

- People who constantly compare themselves to others may experience jealousy when they perceive themselves as less successful or fortunate.

- Example: A family member who makes critical comments about your achievements may be comparing their life to yours and feeling inadequate in the process.

4. Unfulfilled Desires and Ambitions

- Unfulfilled desires and ambitions can lead to envy and resentment towards those who have achieved what they want.

- Example: An acquaintance who undermines your career success might harbour unfulfilled career ambitions of their own.

Setting Boundaries and Protecting Your Space

When you're dealing with jealous individuals, setting clear personal boundaries can help protect your emotional well-being.

Here are some effective ways to achieve this.

1. Establish Clear Boundaries

- Communicate your boundaries clearly and assertively to prevent jealous behaviour from affecting you.

- Example: Politely but firmly let a friend know that negative comments about your achievements are not acceptable.

2. Limit Exposure to Toxic Behaviour from Envious People

- Reduce your interactions with individuals who consistently display envious or jealous behaviour.

- Example: Minimize contact with a neighbour who frequently undermines you. You can avoid situations where their envy is most likely to surface to cause you emotional stress.

3. Protect Your Privacy

- Be mindful of the personal information you share with those who might use it to fuel their jealousy.

- Example: Keep details about your achievements or personal life private from those prone to envy and jealousy. In this case, anyone closely related to you must be made to understand that their association with such a toxic individual is not in your best interest.

In the unfortunate event that such close friends or relatives do not take your warnings seriously, your own effort to protect your privacy will not amount to much. This can lead to devastating consequences for your efforts to protect your privacy and succeed in your chosen field.

This is another area that I've had a bitter experience and I'm still living with the consequences.

4. Seek Support from Others

- Surround yourself with supportive, positive individuals who reinforce your boundaries and offer encouragement.

- Example: Share your experiences with a trusted friend, neighbour, colleague or mentor who can provide advice and emotional support.

Communication Strategies and Conflict Resolution

Effective communication and conflict resolution techniques can help manage envy or jealousy. Let's look at some effective ways to make this happen.

1. Use "I" Statements

- Express your feelings using "I" statements to avoid sounding accusatory and to foster constructive dialogue.

- Example: It is better to say "I feel hurt when my achievements are downplayed," than "You're always negative about my success."

2. Practice Active Listening

- Listen actively to the other person's perspective, showing empathy and understanding.

- Example: Allow an envious neighbour or colleague to express their feelings without judgment.

3. Address Issues Directly

- Confront jealous behaviour directly but calmly, focusing on the behaviour rather than the person.

- Example: Tell them something like, "I've noticed that you often make negative comments when I share good news. Can we talk about what's bothering you?"

4. Seek Win-Win Solutions

- Aim for solutions that address the concerns of both parties and strengthen the relationship.

- Example: Actively look for common ground or mutual goals that can help alleviate envy and jealousy and foster collaboration instead.

5. Agree to Disagree

- Recognize that not all conflicts can be resolved, and it's okay to agree to disagree while maintaining respect for each other.

- Example: Learn to accept the fact that a colleague's envy might never change. But you can still agree to maintain professionalism and mutual respect at work despite your irreconcilable differences.

Dealing with Chronic Envy and Jealousy

In cases where envy or jealousy is chronic and persistent, more intensive strategies may be required to manage the relationship effectively.

1. Consistent Boundaries

- Reinforce your boundaries consistently to prevent ongoing envious behaviour from affecting you.

- Example: Continuously remind an envious family member that their negative comments are hurtful and unacceptable.

2. Distance Yourself

- If the jealousy persists despite your efforts, consider distancing yourself from the individual to protect your well-being.

- Example: You can limit contact with a toxic friend, cousin or neighbour who refuses to respect your boundaries and continues to undermine you.

3. Seek Mediation

- In professional settings, seek mediation from a neutral third party, such as a Human Resource Manager or a supervisor, to address envy-related conflicts that make you feel intensely hated by someone.

- Example: Request a mediation session to resolve ongoing conflicts with a hater in your workplace.

4. Prioritize Self-Care

- Focus on your own well-being by engaging in self-care practices that help you manage stress and maintain emotional balance.

- Example: Practicing mindfulness, seeking therapy, or engaging in hobbies can bring you joy and relaxation.

5. Know When to Walk Away

- Recognize when it's time to walk away from a relationship that is consistently harmful due to chronic jealousy or envy.

- Example: You might want to bring an end to a friendship or relationship that continually undermines your happiness and self-esteem despite repeated efforts to resolve the issues.

Case Studies and Personal Stories

Real-life examples can provide insights into dealing with jealous individuals. They have the ability to illustrate further the effectiveness of the various strategies we've seen so far. Look out for as many such examples as you can while drawing inspiration from your own earlier successes.

1. Case Study: Jealousy in the Workplace

- Scenario: Gladys works with Tom, who often criticizes her work and takes credit for her ideas. Gladys realizes Tom's behaviour stems from envy and jealousy.

- Actions Taken: Gladys sets clear boundaries, communicates her feelings using "I" statements, and seeks support from her manager.

- Outcome: With the manager's mediation, Gladys and Tom establish a more respectful working relationship.

2. Case Study: Envy and Jealousy Among Friends

- Scenario: Rotimi notices his friend Bola becoming distant and critical after Rotimi starts a successful business. Bola's envy affects their friendship.

- Actions Taken: Rotimi addresses the issue directly with Bola. He clearly expresses his feelings in an attempt to understand Bola's thinking.

- Outcome: Bola opens up about his insecurities, and they work together to rebuild their friendship. Rotimi provides all the support and encouragement for Bola's own goals.

Section 3: Thriving Amidst Jealousy and Envy

It isn't enough to just deal with or cope with haters. Such negative people will frustrate you and make your entire life miserable if all you do is try to manage and live with them peacefully. You must move a step further to boldly implement actions steps that will help you achieve all that you dream for your life despite the presence of haters

This brings us to Section 3: Thriving Amidst Jealousy and Envy. This section will show you how to turn negativity into motivation, build a supportive network, and focus on bringing your personal goals to reality.

Turning Negativity into Motivation

When you're able to transform negativity from jealous and envious individuals into a source of motivation it can empower you to achieve your goals even much faster.

Take these steps to turn the negative energy coming from toxic and envious people into your building blocks of massive success.

1. Reframe Negative Feedback

- View criticism and negative comments as opportunities for improvement rather than personal attacks.

- Example: If a colleague criticizes your presentation skills, take it as a cue to refine your public speaking abilities and seek constructive feedback.

2. Use Envy as a Benchmark for Success

- Recognize that envy often indicates you are doing something noteworthy or significant.

- Example: When you notice others feeling envious of your achievements, understand it as a sign that you are making impactful progress. So instead of feeling bad, rejoice.

3. Channel Emotions into Action

- Convert feelings of frustration or anger based on what envious people are doing or saying into productive actions that move you closer to your goals.

- Example: If you feel upset about a business competitor's envious behaviour, channel that energy into working harder on your projects or developing new skills.

4. Set Clear Goals and Intentions

- Live intentionally by establishing specific, measurable goals. It will keep you focused and motivated because it reduces the impact of external negativity.

- Example: You can set a goal to complete an online certification course within six months to top up your professional qualifications.

5. Celebrate Small Wins

- Acknowledge and celebrate your achievements, no matter how small. It will keep you motivated with a positive outlook on life. Do not downplay the significance of your small victories and never wait for anyone to approve your achievements.

- Example: Always reward yourself with a treat or a break after completing a challenging task or reaching a milestone.

Building a Supportive Network

Surrounding oneself with a select group of positive, supportive individuals has proven to be one of the best ways to thrive amid envy and jealousy. Here are some tips to help you create a network of supporters and cheerleaders.

1. Proactively Seek Positive Relationships

- Take conscious steps to build relationships with people who tend to encourage and support your growth and success.

- Example: Join professional networks, social clubs, or community groups where members uplift and inspire one another

2. Get Closer to Mentors and Role Models

- Find mentors and role models who can provide guidance, support, and inspiration.

- Example: Seek out experienced professionals in your field who can offer advice and share their own experiences with personal growth in general or dealing with haters and envious people.

3. Engage in Collaborative Activities

- Participate in collaborative projects and activities that foster teamwork and mutual support.

- Example: Find time to work on group projects, volunteer, or join a sports team to build a sense of companionship and collective achievement.

4. Provide Support to Others

This fight to overcome jealousy, envy and hatred must never be focused on yourself only. Remember, the more you give of yourself, the more spiritual blessings you will receive from the Universe.

- Offer support and encouragement to others. It will help in creating a reciprocal network of positivity and progress.

- Example: Joyfully celebrate a friend's achievements. On the other hand, offer them help when they face challenges.

5. Avoid Negative Influences

- Minimize interactions with individuals who consistently display jealousy or negativity.

- Example: Politely distance yourself from toxic colleagues, schoolmates, neighbours or friends who are constantly looking for ways to undermine your confidence and progress.

Focusing on Personal Goals and Self-Affirmation

When you choose to maintain a clear focus on your personal goals while practicing self-affirmation it can help you thrive despite jealousy and envy.

Here are some top tips to help you do this.

1. Set SMART Goals

- Establish Specific, Measurable, Achievable, Relevant, and Time-bound (SMART) goals that provide a clear roadmap for any aspirations you nurse in your life's journey.

- Example: You can set a goal to improve your fitness by exercising three times a week and tracking your progress over three months.

Make sure to write down your goals. I recently observed to my amazement that any goal that I write down I eventually achieve. So make sure you write the big, positive SMART goals down always. Work on them and leave the rest to the Universe, the source of all energy, growth and abundance.

2. Have a Vision Board

- Visualize your goals and dreams by creating a vision board that serves as a daily reminder of your aspirations.

- Example: Using images, quotes, and symbols that represent your goals and placing the vision board where you can see it regularly.

3. Practice Daily Affirmations

- Use positive affirmations to reinforce your self-belief and confidence.

- Example: Start your day with affirmations such as "I am capable of achieving my goals" or "I am deserving of success and happiness."

4. Track Your Progress

- Regularly monitor and document your progress towards your goals to stay motivated and focused.

- Example: Keep a journal or use a goal-tracking app to record milestones and reflect on the path you've chosen for your life.

5. Regularly Reflect on Your Efforts at Personal Growth

- Take time to reflect on your personal growth and achievements, recognizing the progress you've made.

- Example: You can set aside a weekly or monthly reflection time to review your goals, celebrate successes, and identify areas that need urgent action or improvement.

6. Cultivate a Positive Mindset

- Foster a positive mindset by focusing on gratitude to the Universe, optimism, and resilience.

- Example: Practice gratitude by listing things you are thankful for each day while maintaining a hopeful outlook even in the face of challenges.

Case Studies and Personal Stories

Once again, let's have some case studies to illustrate the above points on how to overcome and thrive in the midst of envious people and haters.

Don't forget that reading or listening to personal stories and case studies can provide valuable insights into how others have thrived amidst jealousy and envy.

1. Case Study: Overcoming Workplace Envy and Jealousy

- Scenario: Valentina is a high-performing employee who often faces envy and jealousy from colleagues. She feels isolated and demotivated by their negative behaviour.

- Actions Taken: Valentina reframes negative feedback and seeks constructive criticism to improve her skills. She also builds a supportive network by finding and working with a mentor. At the same time, she devotes part of her time to engaging in collaborative projects.

- Outcome: Over time, Valentina's performance improves, and she gains recognition for her achievements. Her supportive network helps her navigate envy and jealousy while she maintains focus on her personal goals.

2. Personal Story: Thriving Despite Social Media Envy

- Scenario: Anderson often feels envious when scrolling through social media, seeing friends' glamorous lives. This affects his self-esteem and happiness.

- Actions Taken: Anderson curates his social media feed to follow positive and inspirational accounts. He sets personal goals, practices daily affirmations, and focuses on his own growth.

- Outcome: Anderson's self-esteem improves, and he feels more content and motivated. He builds a network of supportive friends and continues to thrive with his back turned on the faked lives on social media that once triggered feelings of envy in him.

By turning negativity into motivation, building a supportive network, focusing on personal goals and self-affirmation, and implementing long-term strategies, you can thrive amidst jealousy and envy, achieving personal and professional fulfilment.

Section 4: Forgiveness and Letting Go

Our last destination in this chapter is Section 4: Forgiveness and Letting Go. In this section, we will highlight the power of forgiveness in overcoming envy and jealousy. I will provide you with techniques for letting go of grudges. Finally, I will share with you some practical stories of transformation.

The Power of Forgiveness in Overcoming Envy and Jealousy

Forgiveness is a transformative process that can free you from the emotional burdens of jealousy and envy. It involves letting go of resentment and finding peace within yourself.

1. What Is Forgiveness?

- Forgiveness is a conscious decision to release feelings of resentment or vengeance towards someone who has hurt you.

- Example: Forgive a friend, a brother, a partner or a neighbour who undermined your success out of envy or jealousy. This is not to condone their despicable actions but to free yourself from the emotional weight.

2. Benefits of Forgiveness

- Forgiveness promotes emotional healing. It reduces stress and improves the overall well-being of the one who lets go of past hurts.

- Example: Studies show that individuals who practice forgiveness experience lower levels of anxiety and depression, and higher levels of self-esteem and life satisfaction.

3. Treat Forgiveness as Your Chosen Personal Journey

- Forgiveness is more about your healing process than the other person's actions or acknowledgement. When you forgive, it doesn't make the other person a winner and you a loser. In fact, in many cases, it is the other way around.

- Example: Even if the person who hurt you doesn't apologize, choosing to forgive can help you find inner peace. This will empower you to now move forward with your life.

Techniques for Letting Go of Grudges

Letting go of grudges involves actively releasing negative emotions and replacing them with positive ones. Here are some effective techniques:

1. Practice Self-Compassion

- Be kind to yourself and recognize that holding onto grudges can be harmful to your well-being.

- Example: Treat yourself with the same compassion you would offer a friend in a similar situation.

2. Engage in Mindfulness and Meditation

- Mindfulness and meditation can help you stay present and reduce the emotional intensity of grudges.

- Example: Practice mindfulness meditation to observe your thoughts and feelings without judgment, allowing them to pass naturally.

3. Rewrite Your Narrative

- Reframe the story you tell yourself about the event or person who hurt you. Do it in a constructive manner that helps heal your wounds and makes you a better person.

- Example: Instead of viewing yourself as a victim, see yourself as a survivor who has learned valuable lessons and grown stronger.

4. Express Your Emotions

- Find healthy ways to express and release your emotions, such as journaling, talking to a trusted friend, or engaging in creative activities.

- Example: You can write a letter to the person who hurt you (without sending it) to express your feelings and then ceremonially let it all go.

5. Seek Professional Help

- Consider therapy or counselling to work through deep-seated grudges and develop effective coping strategies.

- Example: A therapist can provide tools and techniques to help you process and release negative emotions healthily.

Practical Personal Stories of Transformation

Find and read (or watch) real-life examples of forgiveness and letting go. Such stories can give inspiration as they demonstrate the transformative power of these practices.

Let's have a few examples.

1. Personal Story: Forgiving a Betrayal

- Scenario: Jabulile was deeply hurt when her close friend, Nandi, spread false rumours about her out of jealousy. Jabulile struggled with anger and resentment for months.

- Forgiveness Process: Jabulile sought therapy, practised mindfulness, and engaged in self-reflection to understand Nandi's motives and her own feelings.

- Outcome: Over time, Jabulile chose to forgive Nandi, not to excuse her behaviour but to free herself from the burden of resentment. Jabulile felt a sense of relief and emotional liberation. This helps her to move forward and focus on positive relationships.

2. Personal Story: Letting Go of Professional Jealousy

- Scenario: Oliver was envious of his colleague, Julia, who received a promotion he had been vying for. His jealousy affected his work performance and mental health.

- Letting Go Process: Oliver decided to confront his feelings through journaling and sought mentorship to improve his skills. He also practised gratitude for his current achievements.

- Outcome: Oliver let go of his jealousy, recognizing that Julia's success didn't diminish his own potential. He redirected his energy towards his professional growth, eventually earning a promotion and building a healthier work environment.

Steps to Practice Forgiveness and Letting Go

Here are actionable steps to help you practice forgiveness and let go of negative emotions:

1. Acknowledge Your Emotions

- Recognize and accept your feelings of hurt, anger, or jealousy without judgment.
- Example: Take time to sit with your emotions and understand their origins.

2. Make a Conscious Decision to Forgive
- Decide to forgive, understanding that it is a process that takes time and effort.
- Example: Set an intention to forgive and remind yourself of this decision regularly.

3. Develop Empathy
- Try to understand the perspective and motivations of the person who hurt you.
- Example: Consider the possibility that their actions were driven by their own insecurities and struggles.

4. Release Resentment
- Actively work on releasing feelings of resentment. Go a step further to replace such feelings with positive emotions.
- Example: Visualize letting go of negative emotions and fill the space with peace and compassion.

5. Focus on the Present and Future
- Redirect your focus from the past hurt to your present and future well-being.
- Example: Set new goals. Engage in activities that bring joy and fulfilment to you.

6. Seek Closure
- Find a way to achieve closure, whether through a conversation, a symbolic act, or personal reflection.
- Example: Have a heart-to-heart conversation with the person who hurt you. You can also perform a ritual to signify letting go.

The Long-Term Benefits of Forgiveness and Letting Go

Practicing forgiveness and letting go offers long-term benefits that enhance your overall quality of life. This is why you need to make this choice to help you deal decisively with feelings of envy and jealousy.

Here are some of the greatest benefits to derive from letting go of past hurts to focus on positive directions for your future.

1. Improved Mental Health

- Forgiveness reduces stress, anxiety, and depression. It will help you achieve a better mental health.

- Example: You will feel a sense of relief and lightness after letting go of long-held grudges.

2. Enhanced Relationships

- Letting go of jealousy and resentment fosters healthier, more supportive relationships.

- Example: You will build stronger bonds with friends and family by moving past conflicts and misunderstandings.

3. Greater Emotional Resilience

- Practicing forgiveness enhances your emotional resilience. It will enable you to handle future challenges with grace.

- Example: When you let go, you can develop the ability to bounce back from setbacks.

4. Increased Personal Growth

- Forgiveness allows you to focus on personal growth and self-improvement without being held back by past hurts.

- Example: Beyond forgiveness, you can now direct your energy into pursuing your passions and achieving your goals.

5. Inner Peace and Fulfilment

- Letting go of negative emotions leads to inner peace and a greater sense of fulfilment.

- Example: You can begin to experience a profound sense of contentment and harmony in your life.

It is possible to overcome envy, jealousy and hatred when you choose to forgive. Additionally, adopting the above techniques to let go of grudges, will allow you to turn your back on feelings of resentment. These should enable you to achieve emotional healing and personal growth. This transformative process allows you to move forward with a renewed sense of peace and purpose. The ultimate effect is improved overall well-being and quality of life.

In Chapter 5, the final chapter, you will discover long-term strategies for a jealousy-free, envy-free life

As usual, this chapter is divided into sections. It begins with Section 1: Building Emotional Resilience, you will find daily practices for maintaining emotional health, mindfulness, and stress reduction techniques, and emphasize the importance of creating a positive and affirming environment.

LET'S CONTINUE TO CHAPTER 5: LONG-TERM STRATEGIES FOR A JEALOUSY-FREE, ENVY-FREE LIFE

Chapter 5: Long-Term Strategies for a Jealousy-Free, Envy-Free Life

Short-term measures provide a quick solution when you need to overcome envy and jealousy in all its forms and manifestations. However, you also need strategies to effectively eliminate these emotions from your relationships in the long term. This is what this chapter is all about.

Here is a quick look at the steps anyone who is battling with envy and jealousy needs to adopt for lasting freedom from such emotions whether they exhibit them personally or they are victims looking for redemption.

- The Need to Build Emotional Resilience
- Cultivating Gratitude and Positivity
- Support Others to Conquer Envy and Jealousy
- Moving Forward – A Life Beyond Envy and Jealousy

Section 1: The Need to Build Emotional Resilience

The significance of emotional resilience in the life of every individual cannot be overemphasized. An emotionally balanced individual is better positioned to handle the challenges and stresses that come with today's way of life. Such a person is better equipped to resist the urge to feel envious of others in our present hyper-competitive society. They are also well-placed to deal constructively and decisively with envious people and haters around them.

Building emotional resilience involves adopting daily practices that enhance emotional well-being and prepare you to handle stress and challenges like a pro.

Daily Practices for Maintaining Emotional Health

1. Mindfulness and Meditation

- Practicing mindfulness and meditation helps you stay present and manage stress.

- Example: Start your day with a 10-minute mindfulness meditation to centre yourself and reduce anxiety.

2. Gratitude Journaling

- Keeping a gratitude journal shifts your focus from negative to positive experiences.

- Example: Write down three things you are grateful for each evening before bed. This should help you cultivate a positive mindset.

3. Regular Physical Activity

- Regular physical activity boosts mood and reduces stress.

- Example: Consider incorporating a daily walk, yoga session, or workout routine to improve your physical and mental health.

4. Healthy Eating Habits

- Consuming a balanced diet rich in nutrients supports overall well-being.

- Example: Eat a variety of fruits, vegetables, whole grains, and lean proteins to maintain energy and mental clarity.

5. Adequate Sleep

- Get enough sleep each day. It is crucial for emotional health.

- Example: You can establish a bedtime routine that allows for 7-9 hours of quality sleep each night.

6. Social Connections

- When you keep strong social connections it can provide emotional support since it reduces feelings of isolation.

- Example: Regularly reach out to friends and family, join clubs or groups, and participate in community activities.

Mindfulness and Stress Reduction Techniques

Practice mindfulness and other stress reduction techniques to help you build emotional resilience and manage daily stressors effectively.

Here are a few ideas to guide you.

1. Deep Breathing Exercises

- Deep breathing exercises can quickly reduce stress and calm your nerves.

- Example: Consider practising the 4-7-8 breathing technique: inhale for 4 seconds, hold for 7 seconds, and exhale for 8 seconds.

2. Progressive Muscle Relaxation

- Progressive muscle relaxation involves tensing and then relaxing each muscle group to release tension.

- Example: You can start with your toes and work up to your head, tense each muscle group for 5 seconds, then release.

3. Guided Imagery

- Guided imagery involves visualizing peaceful scenes to promote relaxation that reduces stress.

- Example: Listen to a guided imagery recording that takes you through a serene nature scene to calm your mind.

4. Mindful Walking

- Mindful walking combines movement with mindfulness, helping you stay in the present as a way of reducing stress.

- Example: You can take a walk in nature. Remember to pay attention to the sights, sounds, and sensations around you.

5. Body Scan Meditation

- Body scan meditation helps you become aware of physical sensations and release tension.

- Example: You can lie down and mentally scan your body from head to toe. In the process, notice any areas of tension and consciously relax them.

Create a Positive and Clutterless Environment

Your environment plays a significant role in your emotional resilience. For that matter, creating a positive and affirming environment can enhance your well-being and your emotional health. Take these steps to achieve this.

1. Declutter and Organize

- A clean, organized and minimalist space can reduce stress and promote a sense of calm.

- Example: Regularly declutter your home and workspace. Keep only items that serve a purpose and bring you joy.

2. Incorporate Natural Elements

- Bringing natural elements into your environment can boost the mood thereby reducing stress.

- Example: Add plants, natural light, and nature-inspired decor to your living space.

3. Create a Relaxation Zone

- Designating a specific area for relaxation and self-care can help you unwind and recharge.

- Example: Set up a cosy corner with comfortable seating, soft lighting, and calming music or books.

4. Surround Yourself with Positivity

- Fill your environment with positive affirmations, inspirational quotes, and images that uplift you.

- Example: You can display affirmations on your bathroom mirror or workstation to remind you of your strengths and goals.

5. Limit Negative Influences

- Reducing exposure to negative influences, such as toxic relationships or stressful media, will greatly improve your emotional well-being.

- Example: Set clear boundaries with negative individuals. Do not forget to curate your media consumption to include only positive and uplifting content.

Maintaining Emotional Resilience

Remember that building your emotional resilience as a means to overcoming feelings of jealousy and envy should be an ongoing process. It requires developing and maintaining it through commitment and practice.

1. Develop Self-Awareness

- When you cultivate self-awareness it helps you recognize and understand your emotions and reactions better.

- Example: Regularly check in with yourself to assess your emotional state and identify any stressors or triggers that need to be dealt with.

2. Practice Self-Compassion

- Treat yourself with kindness and understanding, especially during difficult times.

- Example: Acknowledge your efforts and progress. Even if things don't go as planned try to avoid unhealthy self-criticism.

3. Set Realistic Goals

- To stay focused and motivated, always set goals that are realistic and achievable.

- Example: It helps to break larger goals into smaller, manageable steps. Do not forget to celebrate each accomplishment along the way.

4. Welcome Change and Adapt

- Being open to change will make you adaptable to new situations. This is one more way of strengthening your resilience.

- Example: Rather than seeing them as unsurmountable obstacles, consider the challenges in your life as opportunities for learning and growth because that is what they are.

5. Seek Support Each Time You Need It

- Don't hesitate to seek support from friends, family, or professionals when needed.

- Example: Step out and reach out to a therapist or counsellor if you're struggling with persistent stress or emotional difficulties.

6. Maintain a Positive Outlook

- A positive outlook on all the things you go through will help you approach challenges with optimism and resilience.

- Example: It is better to focus on solutions rather than problems. Also, practising gratitude can shift your perspective regarding the things you go through.

Case Studies and Personal Stories

Personal stories and case studies can illustrate how daily practices, mindfulness, and a positive environment contribute to building sustainable emotional resilience. So look out for as many as you can. One place to find these inspiring stories is YouTube. Facebook and Instagram also feature personal stories that help individuals going through difficult moments to pause and reflect.

Let's have a couple of examples.

1. Case Study: Building Resilience After a Job Loss

- Scenario: Rodriguez lost his job unexpectedly and felt overwhelmed by stress and uncertainty.

- Actions Taken: Rodriguez practised mindfulness meditation, engaged in physical activity, and sought support from friends and family. He also created a positive home environment by decluttering and adding natural elements.

- Outcome: Rodriguez developed greater emotional resilience. This enables him to stay positive and focused during his job search. He eventually found a new position that aligned with his goals and values.

2. Personal Story: Overcoming Chronic Stress

- Scenario: Fatima struggled with chronic stress due to a demanding job and personal responsibilities.

- Actions Taken: Fatima incorporated practices such as gratitude journaling, mindful walking, and setting realistic goals in her daily routine. She also created a relaxation zone in her home and limited exposure to negative influences.

- Outcome: Fatima's stress levels decreased, and she felt more balanced and resilient. She was able to manage her responsibilities more effectively and maintain a positive outlook on life.

To summarize, adopting daily practices for emotional health, practicing mindfulness and stress reduction techniques, and creating a positive and affirming environment, will help you build and maintain emotional resilience that can withstand envy, jealousy and hate. This resilience will empower you to handle life's challenges with grace and confidence knowing that, after all, you've been doing quite well.

It's time to move to the next section in this chapter: Cultivating Gratitude and Positivity. Here, we will explore the role of gratitude in reducing envy, introduce positive psychology practices, and share success stories and inspirational quotes to keep you constantly motivated.

Are you ready? Let's do it.

Section 2: Cultivating Gratitude and Positivity

So what is gratitude and what role can it play in reducing the dark emotions of envy, jealousy and outright hatred against others?

The Cambridge Dictionary defines gratitude as *a strong feeling of appreciation to someone or something for what the person has done to help you*.

Thus, gratitude is essentially an expression of thankfulness and an acknowledgement that the Universe has given you and will continue to give you all the things you truly need to have a fulfilling life. Do not forget that the Universal Laws are forever working through individuals to bring us the blessings we often fail to see for what they are, let alone appreciate.

The Role of Gratitude in Reducing Envy and Jealousy

Gratitude has always been a powerful tool for counteracting feelings of envy and jealousy. A thankful attitude enables you to focus on and appreciate what you have, rather than what you lack. Thus, gratitude can shift your perspective and allow you to nurture a mindset of abundance and contentment no matter your circumstances.

1. Shifting Focus

- Gratitude helps shift your focus from envy-inducing comparisons to appreciating your own blessings and achievements.

- Example: Instead of feeling envious of a friend's promotion, you can choose to reflect on and appreciate your supportive family, your sound health or the bright sunny morning peeping through the bedroom window.

2. Enhancing Well-Being

- An enduring attitude of gratitude enhances overall well-being. It produces greater happiness and reduces negative emotions.

- Example: A constant expression or feeling of gratitude has been shown to increase life satisfaction and reduce stress and depression.

3. Fostering Positive Relationships

- Gratitude strengthens relationships as it fosters positive interactions. This is because gratitude is good at reducing feelings of resentment, envy and jealousy.

- Example: When you express gratitude towards your friends and family members for their support, it can enhance your relationships and create a more positive environment.

Positive Psychology Practices

Incorporating positive psychology practices such as the ones below into your daily routine is another way to cultivate a positive mindset that shuns envy and jealousy.

1. Gratitude Journaling

- Write down things you are grateful for each day. Such a daily habit is an effective means to maintain a positive outlook on life despite the challenges.

- Example: You can list three things you are thankful for each morning. They may be a beautiful sunrise, a pleasant surprise, a kind gesture, or a personal accomplishment.

2. Acts of Kindness

- Performing acts of kindness can boost your mood and foster a sense of connection and empathy.

- Example: Volunteer at a local charity, help a needy neighbour with groceries, or simply compliment a colleague for doing something you consider amazing.

3. Positive Visualization

- Visualizing positive outcomes and experiences can enhance your mood and increase motivation.

- Example: Take a few minutes each day to visualize achieving your goals and the positive emotions associated with those achievements.

4. Mindfulness Meditation

- Practicing mindfulness meditation helps you stay present and reduce negative thoughts and emotions.

- Example: Engage in a daily mindfulness meditation session to observe your thoughts and feelings without judgment.

5. Affirmations

- Using positive affirmations can reinforce a positive self-image and boost confidence.

- Example: Each day, repeat envy and jealousy-busting affirmations such as "I am capable and unstoppable", "I am favoured" or I attract positivity and success".

Success Stories and Inspirational Quotes

Learning from others' experiences or reflecting on inspirational quotes can provide motivation and guidance we need to cultivate a mindset of gratitude and positivity.

Here are samples of such soul-inspiring stories you may be familiar with. You can find expanded versions of many such stories in biographies, memoirs, YouTube videos and some personal blogs.

1. Success Story: Overcoming Professional Envy

- Scenario: Esi felt envious of her colleague, who received a prestigious award. This envy affected her performance and relationships at work.

- Actions Taken: Esi began a gratitude journaling practice. Additionally, she performed regular acts of kindness, such as helping colleagues with their tasks. She also used positive affirmations and found inspirational quotes to boost her self-esteem.

- Outcome: Esi's envy diminished, and she felt more content and motivated. Her relationships at work improved, and she eventually received recognition for her efforts.

2. Success Story: Transforming Social Media Envy

- Scenario: John frequently felt envious when scrolling through social media, seeing his friends' seemingly perfect lives.

- Actions Taken: John decided to limit his social media use and focus on positive visualization and gratitude journaling. He also practised mindfulness to stay present and appreciate his own experiences.

- Outcome: John's envy decreased, and he felt more satisfied with his life. He used social media more mindfully, focusing on positive connections and inspiration.

3. Inspirational Quotes

- "Gratitude turns what we have into enough." – Anonymous

- "The more you praise and celebrate your life, the more there is in life to celebrate." – Oprah Winfrey

- "Happiness cannot be travelled to, owned, earned, worn, or consumed. Happiness is the spiritual experience of living every minute with love, grace, and gratitude." – Denis Waitley

- "Gratitude is not only the greatest of virtues but the parent of all others." – Marcus Tullius Cicero

- "The roots of all goodness lie in the soil of appreciation for goodness." – Dalai Lama

Make sure to add to these quotes to give you the strength to overcome needless envy and jealousy.

Implementing a Gratitude Practice

A consistent gratitude practice can help you maintain a positive outlook and reduce feelings of envy. Find below examples of gratitude practice.

1. Daily Gratitude Ritual

- Incorporate a daily gratitude ritual into your routine, such as writing in a gratitude journal or sharing your gratitude with a loved one.

- Example: You can spend a few minutes each morning or evening reflecting on what you are grateful for and writing it down in a journal.

2. Gratitude Jar

- Create a gratitude jar where you can write down things you are thankful for on slips of paper and collect them over time.

- Example: Each day, write down one thing you are grateful for and place it in the jar. Read the slips periodically to remind yourself of your blessings.

3. Gratitude Letters

- Write letters of gratitude to people who have positively impacted your life, expressing your appreciation.

- Example: Write a letter to a mentor, friend, or family member to thank them for their support and kindness.

4. Mindful Appreciation

- Practice mindful appreciation by consciously acknowledging and savouring positive experiences as they occur.

- Example: Taking a moment to fully appreciate a delicious meal, a beautiful sunset, or a kind gesture from a stranger.

5. Share Gratitude

- Share your gratitude with friends, co-workers and siblings to spread positivity and strengthen your relationships.

- Example: You can initiate a tradition of sharing something you are grateful for at family dinners or team meetings.

In effect, cultivating a mindset of gratitude and positivity through daily practices, positive psychology techniques, and learning from inspirational stories and quotes, can reduce feelings of envy. Further, it will lead to a more content and fulfilling life. Remember that these practices will help you maintain a positive outlook, build emotional resilience and, ultimately, improve your quality of life.

Next is Section 3 of this chapter: Supporting Others in Overcoming Jealousy. We will devote our attention to additional long-term methods of overcoming envy and jealousy such as being a role model, offering support and guidance, and creating a community of positive reinforcement.

Section 3: Support Others to Conquer Envy and Jealousy

There are several ways to support others who are battling with envy and jealousy either as perpetrators or as victims. Your ability to help others deal with the problem will, in many ways, reinforce your resilience against these emotions. So let's find out how you can do this.

Being a Role Model for Others

To help others overcome jealousy, it's essential to lead by example. Your actions and attitudes can inspire others to adopt healthier behaviours and mindsets.

1. Exhibit Humility and Gratitude

- Show humility in your achievements and express gratitude for your blessings. This way, many people will have no cause to be envious or hate you.

- Example: When you receive a promotion, acknowledge the support of your team and express gratitude for the opportunities you've had. Avoid the temptation to gloat and spite those you consider your detractors. Let everyone share in your joy of accomplishment.

2. Practice Empathy and Compassion

- Be empathetic and compassionate towards others. Rather than adopt a critical and condescending attitude, show that you understand their struggles and offer support.

- Example: When a friend expresses jealousy, listen without judgment and share your own experiences to help them feel understood.

3. Celebrate Others' Successes

- Actively celebrate and support the successes of others. Show that there is enough success to go around because, truly, there is.

- Example: Congratulate a colleague on their achievements and offer genuine praise and encouragement.

4. Maintain a Positive Attitude

- Cultivate and display a positive attitude. Learn to focus on the good, rather than the bad, in situations and people.

- Example: When faced with setbacks, demonstrate resilience and optimism. Go a step further to encourage others to adopt a similar mindset.

Offer Support and Guidance

Providing support and guidance can help others deal with their feelings of envy and jealousy as they develop more helpful coping mechanisms.

1. Develop a Habit of Active Listening

- Listen actively to others when they share their feelings. Instead of condemnation, give them a non-judgmental listening ear.

- Example: Allow a friend to vent their frustrations and feelings of envy without interrupting or offering immediate solutions. This approach helps heal emotional wounds.

2. Share Personal Experiences

- Share your own experiences with jealousy and how you overcame them, providing relatable and practical advice. Remember not to come across as boastful and unfeeling.

- Example: Discuss a time when you felt envious and the steps you took to address those feelings constructively.

3. Encourage Self-Reflection

- Help others reflect on their feelings and identify the underlying causes of their envy, jealousy or hatred.

- Example: Ask questions that prompt self-reflection, such as, "What do you think triggers these feelings?" or "How can you shift your focus to your achievements?"

4. Suggest Practical Strategies

- Offer the practical strategies we've identified for managing jealousy, such as mindfulness practices, gratitude journaling, and setting personal goals.

- Example: Recommend to your friend or colleague to consider keeping a gratitude journal or practising deep breathing exercises to manage their feelings of envy toward someone.

5. Provide Resources

- If possible, share resources such as books, articles, and workshops that can help others learn more about managing jealousy and building resilience.

- Example: Suggest reading a book like "The Gifts of Imperfection" by Brené Brown or attending a mindfulness workshop.

Create a Community of Positive Reinforcement

A supportive community where positive reinforcement is the norm can help individuals overcome unhelpful emotions such as envy, jealousy and hate. It will also go a long way to promote mutual growth.

Here are some suggestions to let this become a reality.

1. Actively Promote a Supportive Environment

- Create an environment where individuals feel safe to share their feelings and support one another.

- Example: You can help establish regular check-ins or support groups where members can discuss their challenges and successes openly. A well-structured and effectively moderated Facebook Group, for example, is a great fit for this.

2. Promote Collaborative Success

- Encourage collaboration and teamwork, highlighting the value of shared success over individual competition.

- Example: Organize team-building activities and collaborative projects that emphasize collective achievements.

3. Celebrate Achievements Together

- Regularly celebrate the achievements of community members. Build a culture of mutual support and recognition.

- Example: You can host celebratory events or recognition ceremonies to acknowledge individual and group accomplishments.

4. Encourage Positive Communication

- Promote positive and constructive communication within the community while at the same time discouraging gossip and negative talk.

- Example: Draw and implement promptly guidelines for respectful communication and address any instances of negative behaviour.

5. Mentorship Programs

- Establish mentorship programs where experienced members can guide and support others in their personal and professional growth.

- Example: Pair junior employees with senior mentors to provide guidance, support, and encouragement.

Case Studies and Personal Stories

Below are some real-life examples that will illustrate how supporting others can play a vital role in their effort to overcome envy and jealousy.

1. Case Study: Workplace Mentorship

- Scenario: In a competitive corporate environment, Monica noticed her team members often felt jealous of each other's successes.

- Actions Taken: Monica introduced a mentorship program, pairing experienced employees with newer team members. She also organized regular team-building activities and created a recognition program to celebrate individual and team achievements.

- Outcome: The team's morale and productivity improved significantly. Employees felt more supported and valued, reducing feelings of jealousy and fostering a collaborative culture.

2. Personal Story: Community Support Group

- Scenario: William struggled with feelings of envy towards his friends' career advancements and personal achievements.

- Actions Taken: William joined a local support group where members shared their experiences and provided mutual support. He also started practising gratitude journaling and mindfulness meditation, as suggested by the group.

- Outcome: Consequently William's feelings of envy diminished as he focused more on his own growth and the support of his community. He developed stronger, more positive relationships and found greater satisfaction in his own achievements.

Long-Term Strategies for Building a Supportive Community

To ensure the long-term success of a supportive community, it's important to implement strategies that promote continuous growth and positive reinforcement.

1. Regularly Assess Community Needs

- Continuously assess the needs of the community and adopt strategies to meet those needs.

- Example: Conduct surveys or feedback sessions to understand what members find helpful and what must be improved.

2. Encourage Ongoing Learning and Development

- Promote opportunities for continuous learning and development within the community.

- Example: Organize workshops, seminars, and training sessions on topics related to personal growth, emotional resilience, and positive communication.

3. Recognize and Address Challenges

- Proactively recognize and address any challenges or conflicts within the community to maintain a positive environment.

- Example: Implement conflict resolution processes. Do not hesitate to provide mediation services when necessary.

4. Foster Inclusivity and Diversity

- Ensure the community is inclusive and diverse. Value different perspectives and experiences.

- Example: Start initiatives that promote diversity and inclusion. Ensure all members feel welcome and valued.

5. Promote a Culture of Continuous Improvement

- Encourage a culture of continuous improvement, where members are motivated to grow and develop together.

- Example: Celebrate milestones and progress. Then set new goals to keep the community engaged and motivated.

From becoming a role model to giving genuine support, and creating a community of positive reinforcement, you can help others overcome jealousy. These strategies will not only benefit individuals but also strengthen the entire community.

Section 4: Moving Forward: A Life Beyond Jealousy and Envy

Here now comes Section 4: Moving Forward: A Life Beyond Jealousy. This segment will help you set long-term goals for personal and professional growth. We will also emphasize the need to accept change and continuous improvement.

Long-Term Goals for Personal and Professional Growth

To be able to put behind you the burdens of envy and jealousy you ought to set clear, long-term goals that focus on your personal and career development. These goals should be aligned with your values and aspirations so they can give you the needed direction and motivation.

Here are some key steps others have taken to achieve this. I trust that they will work for you too.

1. Identify Your Core Values

- Knowing your core personal values helps you set meaningful goals that align with your true self.

- Example: If integrity and creativity are your core values, set goals that reflect these. Your goals may include pursuing a career in a field that values ethical behaviour and innovation. Such a career will give you maximum satisfaction and fulfilment.

2. Create a Vision Statement

- A vision statement brings together your long-term aspirations. It serves as a guiding star for your goals.

- Example: Someone's vision statement is: "To lead a fulfilling life that balances professional success with personal happiness, continuously learning and growing along the way."

3. Set SMART Goals

The importance of SMART goals in all this cannot be overemphasized. We've already mentioned it elsewhere but it needs repetition here.

- Ensure your goals are Specific, Measurable, Achievable, Relevant, and Time-bound.

- Example: Someone's SMART Goal sounds like this: to become a certified project manager within the next year by completing relevant coursework and passing the certification exam.

4. Break Down Goals into Actionable Steps

- Divide larger goals into smaller, manageable tasks to maintain momentum and track progress.

- Example: Breaking down the goal of starting a business into steps like market research, writing a business plan, securing funding, and launching the product.

It is possible to even break each of these down to smaller achievable targets.

5. Regularly Review and Adjust Your Goals

- Periodically review your goals and adjust them as necessary to reflect changes in your priorities or circumstances.

- Example: Set aside time every quarter to assess your progress and make any needed adjustments to your goals.

Accept Change and Continuous Improvement

To effectively overcome jealousy and envy, it is critical to also adopt a mindset of continuous improvement and remain open to change.

1. Adopt a Development Mindset

- Embrace the belief that abilities and intelligence can be developed through sustained effort and continuous learning.

- Example: Learn to view challenges as opportunities to grow rather than as obstacles to success.

2. Seek Feedback and Learn from It

- Actively seek feedback from others and use it constructively to improve and grow.

- Example: Ask for feedback on a project at work and use the insights to enhance future performance.

3. Stay Open to New Experiences

- When you are open to new experiences and are willing to step out of your comfort zone there's hardly anything that can stop you from achieving sustainable long-term personal growth.

- Example: Don't be afraid to take on new responsibilities at work or try a new side hustle or hobby.

4. Commit to Lifelong Learning

- Continuously seek opportunities for learning and self-improvement.

- Example: You can enrol in online courses, attend workshops and webinars, or read books on topics that interest you.

5. Reflect on Your Progress

- Take time to regularly reflect on your progress. We've already talked several times about the need to celebrate your achievements, no matter how small.

- Example: Keep a journal to document your growth and accomplishments. Review it periodically to stay motivated.

Final Thoughts

As you move forward, remember that overcoming jealousy is a journey, not a destination. It requires patience, self-compassion, and sustained continuous effort. Here are my final words of encouragement to you. They will keep you motivated and strong in your quest for a jealousy-free, envy-free and hate-free life.

Much of these are a recap of some of the most important tips we've identified in our discussion.

1. Practice Self-Compassion

- Be kind to yourself and recognize that overcoming envy, jealousy and hatred is a process that takes time.

- Example: Acknowledge your progress and forgive yourself for any setbacks along the way.

2. Focus on Your Unique Journey

- Remember that in this life, everyone's path is different. This is why you must never lose focus on your path. Always resist the temptation to compare yourself to others.

- Example: Keep recognizing the significance of your unique achievements and milestones, regardless of how they compare to others'.

3. Surround Yourself with Positivity

- Build a support network of positive, encouraging individuals who uplift and inspire you. This cannot be emphasized enough.

- Example: Seek out friends, mentors, and communities that share your values and support your growth.

4. Celebrate Your Successes

- Take time to celebrate your successes and acknowledge the hard work and effort that went into achieving them.

- Example: Reward yourself for reaching a significant milestone or accomplishing a challenging goal.

5. Stay Resilient and Persistent

- Cultivate resilience and persistence. Acknowledge the fact that setbacks are a natural part of life.

- Example: Maintain a positive outlook and, even in the face of daunting obstacles stick to the tasks that move you towards your goals.

6. Enjoy the Process

- Find happiness and satisfaction in your pursuit of personal and professional growth. Yes, derive equal joy from both the challenges and the triumphs.

- Example: You can find joy and fulfilment in the process of learning, growing, and achieving your goals.

Inspirational Poem

Let's end it all with this poem by Rudyard Kipling:

If...

If you can keep your head when all about you
Are losing theirs and blaming it on you,
If you can trust yourself when all men doubt you,
But make allowance for their doubting too;
If you can wait and not be tired by waiting,
Or being lied about, don't deal in lies,
Or being hated, don't give way to hating,
And yet don't look too good, nor talk too wise:

If you can dream—and not make dreams your master;
If you can think—and not make thoughts your aim;
If you can meet with Triumph and Disaster
And treat those two impostors just the same;
If you can bear to hear the truth you've spoken
Twisted by knaves to make a trap for fools,
Or watch the things you gave your life to, broken,
And stoop and build 'em up with worn-out tools:

If you can make one heap of all your winnings
And risk it on one turn of pitch-and-toss,
And lose, and start again at your beginnings
And never breathe a word about your loss;
If you can force your heart and nerve and sinew
To serve your turn long after they are gone,
And so hold on when there is nothing in you
Except the Will which says to them: 'Hold on!'

If you can talk with crowds and keep your virtue,
Or walk with Kings—nor lose the common touch,
If neither foes nor loving friends can hurt you,
If all men count with you, but none too much;
If you can fill the unforgiving minute
With sixty seconds' worth of distance run,
Yours is the Earth and everything that's in it,
And—which is more—you'll be a Man, my son!

Conclusion

Your quest to overcome jealousy, envy and haters is a transformative process that requires self-awareness, resilience, and a commitment to continuous growth. By setting long-term goals, accepting change, and developing a positive mindset, you can create a fulfilling and successful life. Remember to practice self-compassion, focus on your unique journey, and surround yourself with positivity. Also, celebrate your successes and stay resilient in the face of challenges.

Above all, approach all your efforts with an open heart and a positive outlook, bearing in mind that each step you take brings you closer to a life devoid of envy, jealousy and hate

Summary and Key Takeaways

1. Recognize and Understand Envy and Jealousy: Identify the signs and root causes of jealousy and envy in yourself and others.

2. Set Long-Term Goals: Establish clear, meaningful goals that align with your values and aspirations.

3. Embrace Continuous Improvement: Adopt a growth mindset, seek feedback, and stay open to new experiences and learning opportunities.

4. Practice Self-Compassion: Be kind to yourself and recognize that overcoming jealousy is a process that takes time.

5. Focus on Your Unique Story: Celebrate your achievements and focus on your personal growth, rather than comparing yourself to others.

6. Build a Positive Support Network: Surround yourself with supportive, positive individuals who uplift and inspire you.

7. Celebrate Successes: Take time to acknowledge and celebrate your successes and the hard work that went into achieving them.

8. Remain Resilient and Persistent: Cultivate resilience and persistence, knowing that setbacks are a natural part of the endeavour.

9. Enjoy the Process: Cheerfully accept your path to conquer envy, and overcome your haters. Find joy and fulfilment in each step.

Resources and Further Reading

1. Books

- *Unlocking the Secret to Harmonious Relationships* by Joshua J. Griffin

- Summary of Personal Power by Tony Robbins[1]

- *The Gifts of Imperfection* by Brené Brown

- *Mindset: The New Psychology of Success* by Carol S. Dweck

- *The Art of Happiness* by Dalai Lama and Howard Cutler

2. Articles and Online Resources

- Seeds of Success: 20 Top Life Coaches in the World to Follow[2]

- Urban Yogi: Meditation and Sleep App[3]

- 12 Reasons to Stop Living to Impress Others[4]

- Authentic Happiness Website[5]

- The Art and Science of Relationships: Understanding Human Needs (Coursera)[6]

- Rising Above the Noise: 10 Ways to Handle Haters and Jealous Individuals[7]

- MasterClass Self-Improvement Resources[8]

3. Support Groups and Communities

- 10 Online Support Groups for Anyone Struggling Right Now[9]

1. https://bloggingtothemax.com/summary-of-personal-power-by-tony-robbins-pdf/

2. https://bloggingtothemax.com/seeds-of-success-20-top-life-coaches-in-the-world-to-follow/

3. http://appsumo.8odi.net/7525Wy

4. https://bloggingtothemax.com/12-reasons-to-stop-living-to-impress-others-start-living-intentionally/

5. https://www.authentichappiness.sas.upenn.edu/

6. http://imp.i384100.net/vNBPnj

7. https://bloggingtothemax.com/rising-above-the-noise-10-ways-to-handle-haters-and-jealous-individuals/

8. http://masterclass.pxf.io/LPbWX0

- Deciding to Be Better SubReddit[10]
- The Girl Survival Guide SubReddit[11]
- The Tiny Buddha Community [12]

The End

9.   https://www.self.com/story/online-support-groups

10.   https://www.reddit.com/r/DecidingToBeBetter/

11.   https://www.reddit.com/r/TheGirlSurvivalGuide/

12.   https://tinybuddha.com/blog/introducing-tiny-buddhas-community-forums/

Don't miss out!

Visit the website below and you can sign up to receive emails whenever Ralph Nyadzi publishes a new book. There's no charge and no obligation.

https://books2read.com/r/B-A-OQZF-GTARD

BOOKS 2 READ

Connecting independent readers to independent writers.

Also by Ralph Nyadzi

Fast Track WASSCE General Arts
Fast Track WASSCE Government: Elements of Government

Standalone
Regrets
The Self-Support Guide
Becoming Self-Employed
Understanding Grammatical Names and Functions
Second Class Citizen Summary & Analysis
The Lion and the Jewel Summary & Analysis
WAEC Literature Poetry: Summary & Analysis
WAEC Literature African Poetry Summary & Analysis
WAEC Literature Non-African Poetry Summary & Analysis
What Makes A Hater

Watch for more at https://www.cegastacademy.com.

About the Author

Ralph Nyadzi is the founder of **RN Diggital** - a digital publishing and content marketing agency for small local businesses. He teaches English for Academic Purposes (EAP) online and blogs at Cegast Academy and BloggingtotheMax.com. Besides writing full-time, he enjoys cooking and farming. Ralph lives in the coastal belt of Ghana, his native country.

Read more at https://www.cegastacademy.com.

About the Publisher

Cegast Academy is the sole publisher of books authored by Ralph Nyadzi and other authors who are happy to work with him.

Read more at https://www.cegastacademy.com/.